The Library Leader's Guide to Human Resources

The Library Leader's Guide to Human Resources

Keeping it Real, Legal, and Ethical

Steve Albrecht

ROWMAN & LITTLEFIELD
Lanham • Boulder • New York • London

Rowman & Littlefield
Bloomsbury Publishing Inc, 1385 Broadway, New York, NY 10018, USA
Bloomsbury Publishing Plc, 50 Bedford Square, London, WC1B 3DP, UK
Bloomsbury Publishing Ireland, 29 Earlsfort Terrace, Dublin 2, D02 AY28, Ireland
www.rowman.com

86-90 Paul Street, London EC2A 4NE

British Library Cataloguing in Publication Information Available

Library of Congress Cataloging-in-Publication Data

Names: Albrecht, Steve, 1963- author.
Title: The library leader's guide to human resources: keeping it real, legal, and ethical / Steve Albrecht.
Description: Lanham: Rowman & Littlefield, [2025] | Includes bibliographical references and index.
Identifiers: LCCN 2024059378 (print) | LCCN 2024059379 (ebook) | ISBN 9781538193747 (cloth) | ISBN 9781538193754 (paperback) | ISBN 9781538193761 (ebook)
Subjects: LCSH: Library personnel management—United States.
Classification: LCC Z682.2.U5 A43 2025 (print) | LCC Z682.2.U5 (ebook) | DDC 023.0973—dc23/eng/20250212
LC record available at https://lccn.loc.gov/2024059378
LC ebook record available at https://lccn.loc.gov/2024059379

For product safety related questions contact productsafety@bloomsbury.com.

♾TM The paper used in this publication meets the minimum requirements of American National Standard for Information Sciences—Permanence of Paper for Printed Library Materials, ANSI/NISO Z39.48-1992.

Contents

Acknowledgments

Since all the really cool guys are named Steve, I'll start by thanking Steve Hargadon, founder of Library 2.0, and my partner at www.TheSafeLibrary .com.

Steve H. offers wise and thoughtful counsel on all of my library training, writing, and marketing efforts.

Kate Hall, the executive director of the Northbrook, Illinois, Library, is the co-author, along with Kathy Parker, of a mighty fine companion book to mine: *The Public Library Director's HR Toolkit* (2022). Where there are gaps in your knowledge due to my limitations, Kate and Kathy's book should be your additional guide.

Cindy Church, from the State Library of Virginia, has been a boon friend first and a longtime client second. She is a barometer for all things library training, current and future.

Introduction

This book is meant to be equal parts informational and motivational. I wrote it in the first-person to share my experiences as an HR consultant, an employee coach at all levels in many public and private-sector organizations, an expert witness in HR civil cases, and as a personnel management practitioner. I try to cover serious things with a lighter touch.

The contents are equal parts operational, practical, and realistic. I designed this book to resonate with the library director who has full HR responsibilities for her or his library; or the deputy director, assigned to all HR functions, among other logistical or day-to-day tasks; or the sole HR professional in a library or library district, who has to juggle many responsibilities alone. And I'm writing to the HR director or HR manager, who may have HR staff (called HR analysts in some libraries), who can give this book to them to help them grow and develop into their roles as subordinates to HR leaders, which can give the HR leader more time to focus on strategic, longer-term, and leadership projects.

You may take some of my advice for yourself, but if you already know what I'm describing, your greatest effort is to help the bosses at every level in your library branch, district, or system to succeed. Turn what you read here back into your subtle or bold efforts to educate them about what they need to know. You'll see me make frequent use of the phrase "directors, leaders, managers, supervisors, or PICs" to describe the leadership cadre in your library that has supervisory power over their employees. This means they fall under the definition of a boss as being in control of their employees' work duties, work assignments, work schedules, projects, deadlines, outputs, and service interactions with patrons and colleagues. When I am speaking to you, you can take these words and speak to them.

Figure 0.1 Our Library HR Triangle. Steve Albrecht

You may see me refer to "My Perfect HR World," which is where best practices and ideal conditions come together to give you the time, money, expertise, and resources you need to create the HR department you want and your employees will value. Perhaps this HR nirvana is closer to you than you might first think, especially if you grasp the concepts found in the above model.

This triangle with a central focus can help us visualize the important HR functions in your library by thinking first about the critical core activities, which surround our ongoing promise to do everything necessary, ethical, and legal to help us all keep on keeping on. The components are both abstract and necessary to put into concrete, operational actions.

Compass: Setting the direction for our HR functions and our reason for existing: to serve the people side of our enterprise.

Culture: Building a culture of civility, fairness, and equal opportunity which respects the collective diversity of our employees and patrons.

Compliance: We will strive to stay legal and ethical, by partnering with our attorney advisors and keeping up on the changes in the HR world of laws, policies, and guidelines at the federal, state, and local levels.

All of these surround the Commitment we make to support our library, grow the business through selecting new employees and promoting existing ones, and serve every department inside our library and those that support us, like our city and county partners, boards, and elected or appointed officials.

Each of the three elements that support the center element are equally important and need your energy, focus, and support. It's easy to get caught up in the day-to-day small blazes and raging forest fires and lose sight of the Compass and the Culture. It's easy to assume that the Culture will take care of itself and does not need attention, food, and watering (library people love break room cake!). It seems like the Compliance piece gets harder, more complex, more statutorily driven, and less intuitive. But for the laws, policies, exclusions, and prohibitions, it's still a people business. That means the lawyers aren't in the building every morning to run your department; you are.

As just one example of the nonstop complexities of the Compliance portion of HR, the federal Equal Employment Opportunity Commission (EEOC) just came out with a new set of guidelines for sexual and racial harassment prevention in our workplaces. It seems hard to believe, but the last set of rules, instructions, and policy language from them came out in 1999!

So after a twenty-five-year hiatus, on April 29, 2024, the US EEOC has finally released its new guidelines for all employers, to better understand Title VII of the 1964 Civil Rights Act. Their report offers several important new changes as to how employers must classify "legally protected characteristics," like age, race, skin color, pregnancy, lactation, sexual orientation, gender, gender identity, and prohibit mislabeling restrooms or misgendering someone.

The EEOC received over 37,000 comments from the public, businesses, and law firms. They have built a report that features seventy-seven example scenarios of harassment, which cover issues like enforcing policies in a Work From Home (WFH) environment; prohibiting what it calls "intraclass harassment," where someone is harassed by a member of the same protected class; social media account harassment; and even workplace conduct that takes place over video-based meeting and training platforms like Zoom, or MS Teams.

The report also features a few footnotes—only 387 of them—to help you do a deeper dive into the whys and hows. I had flashbacks of going through graduate school again as I read it.

You can find it here: https://www.eeoc.gov/laws/guidance/enforcement -guidance-harassment-workplace.

WE START BY SERVING EACH OTHER (OR WE DON'T)

Can we begin by agreeing on this overarching HR concept?

Excellent internal service to each other leads to excellent external service to our patrons.

And the reason this is true is because there are really only four possibilities in every library work culture:

1. We take really good care of each other; it's a positive, fun place to work and the employees stay, but we don't take care of our patrons, and they complain. (In the old days, they wrote angry letters to the local

newspapers about unprofessional service at the library. Today they complain bitterly on Facebook, X/Twitter, Yelp, etc.)

2. We take really good care of the patrons; they enjoy our best service efforts, but we don't take care of each other as bosses and co-workers. Longtime employees get fed up and leave and it's hard to hire and keep the new ones.

3. We don't take care of the patrons, so they complain to the usual social media sources and to the library board and/or other elected or appointed officials (who don't like to get lumped into stories of poor service to taxpayers). And we don't take care of the employees, so the good ones—who have positive attitudes and a service-first orientation—leave, and the lousy ones stay and continue to mistreat the patrons.

4. The goal and the best of all possible approaches in our Perfect Library World (PLW) is, of course, a staff that takes care of the patrons and each other, in equal measures. I have seen this combination in many libraries and perhaps so have you, and maybe even in your own, today.

If you are in any other territory than Number 4, then we have some work to do to get you to that place. (Library leaders stuck in Number 3 are probably too busy polishing their résumés and looking on job sites to be reading this.)

Where is your library on this list of four? Where do you want it to be?

What are you willing to do to move to the number you want?

BUILDING THE MISSION STATEMENTS OF EACH LIBRARY DEPARTMENT: THE A-B-C APPROACH

In my view, one of the weak links in many city and county agencies is the exalted and often poorly written mission statement. Some of these exist to describe and define the overall city or county philosophy (which includes a long list of platitudes no one—least of all most taxpayers—ever read entirely) and which attempt to espouse the actions of each city or county department.

In my experience in looking at city and county government operations for over thirty-eight years, these word salads are Utterly Joyless, too long, meandering, and seemingly written by robotic bureaucrats rather than actual people.

Two examples make my point and perhaps you have seen likewise where you have worked:

City Parks and Recreation Department #1: "We strive to provide the very best in parks and recreation facilities, programs, events, and services to our community. In doing so, we will make a positive impact on the overall quality of life, health, environmental, social, diversity, and economic aspects for our resident families and visitors alike." (48 words)

City Parks and Recreation Department #2: "We're in the business of fun! We provide the places, programs, and stuff for our citizens and their kids to enjoy themselves!" (22 words)

Which city would you rather work in? Which parks would you rather go to on the weekend?

County Recorder's Office #1: "The Recorder of Deeds is responsible for making record of documents primarily in real estate and the issuance of marriage licenses. In addition, Uniform Commercial Code, servicemen's records, tax liens and miscellaneous documents may be recorded upon request and compliance with statutes. Records in this office provide data about real estate transactions in a historical perspective. Deeds, deeds of trust, releases, easements, surveys, plats, restrictions, cemetery deeds, wills, road right of ways, articles of incorporation, patents, affidavits and marriage license information make up an example of the documents." (88 words)

County Recorder's Office #1: "We store and protect the important historical records for this county, making them available to residents, researchers, and professionals." (19 words)

Again, Example #1 is certainly accurate (if dull), while Example #2 is probably the one the employees who work there can memorize and repeat.

The A-B-C exercise is a useful activity for any city or county leader to do to craft a short, concise, and dare we say, memorable and memorizable mission statement. I have done this dozens of times with the leaders and staff from many city and county departments, and not surprisingly, they often struggle with their results. When I ask them to boil down what they do, who it helps, and who they serve, they can't get all that down to one or two sentences that are both informative and non-bureaucratic.

A library's mission statement is not the same as a vision statement or a library's strategic plan. The former is the ABCs; the second is about goals and how to achieve them; and the third is about the direction for the entire organization.

Consider doing this mission statement exercise for your HR function, whether you're an HR department of one or you're the HR director with a staff. Write a new mission statement for the HR function in your library:

Activities—What do we do?
Benefits—Who does it benefit, inside and outside our department, and in the community we serve?
Customers—Who do we serve?

How did you do? Let's continue our model of Example 1 (bureaucratic, stodgy) and Example 2 (where we might actually want to work):

Example 1: "Our office supports the personnel functions for the library, by screening applicants, conducting interviews, and hiring qualified employees for the various positions we staff. We help the Library Director set policies concerning the management, supervision, discipline, promotions, termination, retirements, and benefits of all employees, through the duration of their employment." (50 words)

Example 2: "We help select and support awesome people who want to work in a library career!" (15 words)

Which library would you want to work at?

THE LONG ROAD TO MORE HR LOVE STARTS WITH YOUR STRATEGIC PLAN

Might we say it has always been and will continue to be challenging to be in the human resources business? We are expected to predict the future: Will this applicant turn into one of our rising star employees or end up suing us five weeks after they quit because they didn't like our attendance policies? We are expected to be predictors of the employee's future, which is not possible or recommended.

I came from a time when HR was still an all-paper business, with files and files of our employees' work histories (thick collections of the good and bad) stored in rows of metal cabinets. Scanning résumés and screening for keywords using hiring software was not common. The Internet was not where we posted for new jobs or promotional opportunities; it was more about bulletin boards and memos passed around at staff meetings. We used job fairs and word-of-mouth recruiting, classified ads, and recruiting posters. An applicant's hand-scrawled job application and/or résumé got a careful or quick review and the interview process ranged from detailed and legal to haphazard and driven by intuition. Sometimes diplomas and certifications were the most important selection criteria; other times it was so-called their time in grade, meaning have they done this exact job, somewhere else, in a reasonably accomplished way? Like now, reference checks were attempted, and not always with much satisfaction with the non-answer answers warily provided by the applicant's former employers. Hiring people back then was often more about their experience than their enthusiasm, which didn't always work out so well.

While I was in graduate school for my master's, I reasoned that having my SHRM certification would be my next goal, so I studied for the test and passed it, earning my PHR certification (Professional in Human Resources) in 1995. The people who earned their SPHR (Senior Professional in Human Resources) usually worked in an HR function for a firm. PHR types like me often became consultants, so that was the path I trod.

I continue to recertify my PHR through SHRM and try to stay up on the HR trends, laws, and obstacles to "better people management." It's certainly reasonable to say the process of employing people is more complex now than when I started thirty years ago. The fear of litigation is ever-present, even though it's still difficult to sue an organization successfully that has followed legal, ethical, and fair guidelines and practices in its efforts to run a public or private sector business in a way that demands accountability, rewards effort, and promotes based on enthusiasm, skill, and hard work.

Yet for all our advances, I still see a ringing phrase in many HR publications, most often in SHRM's HR Management magazine, that sings the same sad song: "How Does HR Get a Chair in the C-Suite?" and "How Does HR Get Invited to the Big Table?"

The variations on this recurring theme are, "Why Don't We Ever Get Invited to Important Strategizing Meetings?" or "How Can We Get the Rest of the Organization to Take HR Seriously?"

Want to know the answer to every variation of that question?

You need to know how and why to tie your efforts in HR to your library's strategic plan (or the strategic plan of your city or county if you are under that umbrella).

Your library's strategic plan ties together the operational, financial, long-term, goals, direction, and solution-oriented efforts, that help to create the workplace culture, which in turn, serves a diverse community.

Your success, long term, in HR, happens best when you use leadership language, not short-term, day-to-day, operational, "managership" language.

And as one longtime CEO told me, HR needs to "Speak the language of business, which means we're all about money. So either help us save it or help us make it, and preferably both."

Don't let other leaders—above your peer level or at it—refer to your department as a "body shop." Some business executives have taken this derogatory phrase to mean, "Just get us the people we need to get the job done. Keep us out of court. We'll let you know if we need you for anything else." This denigrating term should not depict your efforts or the role and function of your HR department.

HAVE WE IMPROVED OUR REPUTATION
IN TWENTY YEARS?

If we turn our way-back machine to August 1, 2005, our eyes will fall upon the cover and supporting article from the business magazine *Fast Company*. Neither the headline nor the story, written by Keith H. Hammonds, sugarcoat things. Anything that starts with "Why We Hate HR" is not going to be a picnic.

The subtitle offers us even less joy: "In a knowledge economy, companies with the best talent win. And finding, nurturing, and developing that talent should be one of the most important tasks in a corporation. So why does human resources do such a bad job—and how can we fix it?"

Hammonds begins his piece: "Well, here's a rockin' party: a gathering of several hundred midlevel human-resources executives in Las Vegas. (Yo, Wayne Newton! How's the 401[k]?) They are here, ensconced for two days at faux-glam Caesars Palace, to confer on 'strategic HR leadership,' a conceit that sounds, to the lay observer, at once frightening and self-contradictory. If not plain laughable.

"Because let's face it: After close to 20 years of hopeful rhetoric about becoming 'strategic partners' with a 'seat at the table' where the business decisions that matter are made, most human-resources professionals aren't nearly there. They have no seat, and the table is locked inside a conference room to which they have no key. HR people are, for most practical purposes, neither strategic nor leaders."[1]

The responses to this article, in the following month, generated a wave of both angry and supportive emails and Letters to the Editor, by readers who completely disagreed with Hammonds' premise and those who thought he was absolutely correct. So much so that the magazine devoted much space in the next month's issue talking about the polarized reactions. As you can already guess, HR professionals were outraged and tried hard to defend their vocation and avocation. But, not surprisingly, because it makes for better reading, at least from the editors' view, that the majority of people who wrote in backed his conclusion. They provided their own stories of the various sins of omission and commission of their own HR departments.

To say the original story and the accompanying howls of both protest and support struck a collective corporate nerve understates it by half. Learn from this perception by the non-HR world and be different in your approach, knowing first that this perception still exists and second, that you can do something about changing it, in large and small ways, throughout your career.

MAKING THE ABSTRACT CONCRETE

Words matter, accuracy should mean something, and descriptions that most people can recognize, agree with, and support are important. The original operational definition of the finding, interviewing, hiring, managing, and/or terminating or retiring of the people needed to operate private-sector companies and public agencies fell to the people operating the "Personnel Department." They worked on "personnel issues" and helped the company leaders, managers, and supervisors stay legal and ahead of "personnel problems." Many of these things were kept in confidence because they were a "personnel matter" (which meant they were best to be kept personal).

While some of my city and county clients still use "Personnel" as their label for the people side of their agencies, the majority of them—and all of my private-sector clients—refer to themselves as operating the "Human Resources Department." Does it really matter what we call ourselves? "Personnel Professional" sounds goofy, right?

Parts of HR, as a process, are abstract; parts are concrete. The abstract parts could refer to fairness, providing opportunities, staying compliant, and following guidelines. The concrete parts should refer to how we are fair, how we provide opportunities, how we stay legal and compliant, and how we follow guidelines. The how part is observable, operational, and visible to others throughout the organization. A policy prohibiting sexual harassment prevention is filled with more abstract language than concrete language; because of the legalities involved, it has to be that way. The introduction, education about, and enforcement of that policy—and any subsequent revisions—needs to be operationalized, and made concrete, so that the people who read it can understand it and follow it, without having to go to law school first. In my view, one of the overarching functions of the modern HR department—and there are a lot—is to make the complexities of that world easy for the employees—at every level—to understand and comply with.

We can find an example of the need to be clear and to move from the abstract language to the operationally concrete in the lobby of a city or county administration building, or even in the break room or the employees-only hallway in your library. How many times have you walked by a motivational poster or more likely, the city or county's "Vision and Values" poster and seen phrases like these below?

Here are two posters from the lobby of my building:

Our Achievements Are Shaped By The Terrain Of Our Lives And The Strength Of The Foundations We Set. In Building The Life We've Imagined, We Must Be True To Our Beliefs, Dare To Be Ethical, And Strive To Be Honorable. For Integrity Is The Highest Ground To Which We Can Aspire.

Sometimes We Learn The Hard Way That It Doesn't Pay To Get Discouraged.
Positive Thinking Is An Intellectual Choice, And By Keeping Our Eyes Focused
On The Light Of Optimism, We Can Restore Faith In Ourselves And Stay Clear
Of The Shadows.

Great! What does all that really cool (motivation-speak, gobbledygook,
work culture, word-salad claptrap) mean, anyway?

It may be true that, "Employees don't quit their jobs, they quit their
bosses." I think that's only partially correct. You can have a lousy boss and
stay for many years, working hard, not for him or her, but for the success of
your own career path, because it supports your colleagues and co-workers,
whom you do like, despite your boss's overall horribleness. It's all about the
work culture. While a bad boss can create a toxic work culture, that ultimately
drives away even the heartiest and most optimistic employee, if the employees create their own successful work culture, which works around their bad
boss, they will stay.

We can see examples of this with winning professional sports teams. While
it's rare and less common than with teams who love their coach, there are
winning teams who have banded together to do well, despite their bad boss.

Employees will quit the culture even when their boss is "an island of nour-
ishment surrounded by a sea of toxicity." A good boss can help a lot, making his or her department or team succeed, but they cannot rescue a terrible
overall culture.

Pay is never the only reason why employees come to work or stay there.
It's certainly a motivating factor, but not the motivating factor. How do we
know this is true? Because many people work for free, donating hundreds of
unpaid hours—at their kid's school, volunteering to run a sports league, for
their church, for a community group, for a political party or a civic cause they
believe in—not for money, status, or power, but because it feels good and it
feels right to them. There is what is written and then there is what is done.

In most government-centered agencies, it's common for longtime or older
employees to take the new hires aside and say, "Yeah, well, what they told
you to do and how we really do things around here are two different things."
There is What the Policy Manual Says and then there is What the Work
Culture the Employees Have Created Says. The wise HR professional knows
how to interpret these gray areas.

Your work culture is a fragile thing, whether it was in place when you
arrived or you have worked hard to build it.

SOME LEADERSHIP TRUTHS

Being a boss now sure looks different than before the pandemic and being an HR boss is even more different/unusual. (Who would have thought we'd ever need to discuss how to have library employees work from home?)

Consider these as our emerging leadership truths:

The higher you get, the less "work" you do. This seems untrue but it just is. Once you promote or rise to the top of your business, you actually get further away from the field. Some employees never want to be promoted because they like working where they are or doing what they're doing and don't want the responsibilities or the pleasures/hassles of supervising their peers. Once you start to move up the ladder, you're doing lots of work to be sure, but it's different work than what you were first hired for or what you started off doing.

There will never be enough time, resources, money, or people to do everything you need to do or want to do. So stop saying, "Where does the time go?" and make better use of the time you have. Free up your time by delegating more. If you're always going home tired and the people who work for you are never going home tired, you need to give them more to do. Budgets are always tight, staffing is rarely at full, and even when you have money and personnel, it doesn't feel like it's enough. Prioritize!

Don't ignore the Strength-Weakness Irony. This is a human trait we all have, a concept some of us understand more intuitively, acutely, and externally than others. And it's one that we don't see in ourselves: "Your strength, taken to an extreme, becomes a weakness." Whatever you're too good at can become a blind spot.

From a work perspective, the Strength-Weakness Irony often manifests itself in a huge time drain for you, where you get tied up in issues, problems, and events that are probably not in your area of responsibility as an HR leader. See if you recognize yourself in some of these:

Workaholism. If I said, "Hi. I'm Steve and I'm a workaholic," some of you might quickly shout "Hi Steve!" which means you're workaholics too. This is not a badge of honor. Even though it might seem like it's good for your career or your bank account, it's really bad for your physical and mental health.

"Super Boss" diesease. "I'll take care of it. I'll handle it. Step aside! Boss coming through." Your strength—you're hands-on—becomes a weakness and you slip into micromanager territory. Super Bosses have difficulty delegating and this leads their employees to believe they are not trusted to do their jobs.

Perfectionism. "I need to make one more tweak to the PowerPoint before I send over the training slides" or "I'll have to go over this staffing report for my library director one more time with a red fine-tooth comb before I email it over." Sometimes, good enough is good enough. Bosses who seek perfection in all they create (and from what they expect from others) will be disappointed. Plus, it's a huge time waster. A CEO I knew was once asked by his staff to pick the trees to be planted in the green areas around the exterior of the building. He carefully researched his answers and provided his choices—two years later.

"I can't say no." This one is often connected to the others. When you demonstrate your workaholic traits to others, when you wear the Super Boss cape, and when you try to be too perfect, you end up taking on other people's work, fail to delegate, and become exhausted. Good HR leaders use their human resources assertively and with compassion; they make the best use of time and people. It's not always about what you can do alone, nor should it be.

Finally, remember Teddy Roosevelt. He said, "Do the best you can, with what you have, where you are." How about we modify his advice slightly, to say, **"Do the best you can, with *who* you have, where you are."** You can't always pick who works for you, but you can pick what they do for you. Make the best fits, between their KSAs (knowledge, skills, abilities) and what needs to get done. Don't hesitate to give your people new challenges, related but different job duties, and opportunities to succeed (or learn by failing, safely). That's how you identify who your future leaders are.

NOTE

1. https://www.fastcompany.com/53319/why-we-hate-hr.

Chapter 1

Navigating the Entire Library Employment Cycle

From Hiring Interviews to Exit Interviews

We can define the employment cycle as every milestone that touches the initial applicant or the subsequent employee, starting with the way we post or recruit for the position; how we have crafted the salary, job duties, job description, and benefits language; the selection process from many to a selected group for in-person, panel, Zoom, or over the phone interviews; and the background screening process. (Don't forget to get the applicant's signed permission to run a credit check if he or she will have fiduciary responsibilities—drafting checks, making deposits—as part of their work.)

Once the employment offer is made, the background checks are completed—and the applicant has had the chance to explain any discrepancy in his or her copy of the written report, as per the Fair Credit Reporting Act (FCRA)—then the onboarding/orientation/new-hire process can begin.

In this chapter, we'll focus on two critical pieces: the beginning—the hiring interview, and the end—the exit interview. Other chapters will look at performance, coaching people up (or out), discipline, termination, and everything in between. For now, let's start our HR journey at the start of the river and end it at the end of the river.

Joining a new organization is exciting and stressful for both sides. The new employee wants—we hope—to make a good first impression, to get enrolled in the various benefits programs, to be made aware of the myriad of policies and procedures for the job, to meet her or his boss and colleagues, and to be given work that is connected to their skill set, education, and experience. In short, nothing overwhelming at the start, but a gradual process that helps them acclimate from day one to the end of their probationary period.

Some organizations do this well and others rush the process, so that the employees feel abandoned, deluged with policy minutiae, and therefore, not connected to the job or their co-workers. This time span is critical because if

13

it's not handled with skill, tact, and patience, the person may swiftly decide that this is the wrong place for them and we are back to sifting through applications.

I have never found an employment situation where the probationary period was not worth the effort. It serves two purposes, and these are not just for the benefit of the employer. It also lets the employee ask themselves, is this the right place for me to stay, grow my career, or should I go elsewhere? It helps management make a legal, ethical decision about keeping the employee or not, which should be a go/no-go decision, not an agonizing struggle.

ROCK-SOLID, LEGAL JOB DESCRIPTIONS AND DUTIES

Keep up-to-date with the socioeconomic trends in your community. This means you should have a fairly accurate assessment of how many dollars it takes to make a living and be able to afford housing, food, transportation, utilities, and daycare in the neighborhoods where your library is and from where you're hiring. I believe in the power of salary survey data, which can tell you how to adjust your wage and salary rates, but more importantly, may help convince those who control your budget dollars—city manager, county administrative officer, CEO, city council members or county supervisors, finance director, or library board—why you need to pay competitive wages to get and keep skilled people in a niched profession that takes certifications, degrees, experience, and talent.

The salary survey process is often conducted by the same types of consultants who can help you fine-tune and improve your job descriptions and job duties for each position in your library, including part-time jobs, internships, and even volunteer positions. Accurate job descriptions and duties help applicants understand what will be required of them and help you craft better interview questions.

And can your library become a positive trendsetter by doing what other public agencies and private sector companies seem so hesitant to do? Which is to provide the salary for the position on all public-facing applications, websites, and job postings. No applicant looks to waste time applying for a job where the salary is a mystery until during the interview or right after the job is offered. The process of applying for a job is stressful, even if you have had experience doing it. It drives me crazy when I see online applications that ask, "What salary or hourly rate will you accept?" What is the applicant supposed to say? "I don't want to say I'll work for $10 per hour but if I put I want $63,000 per year, with medical benefits, will they hire me?"

In not posting the salary or hourly rate, I'm trying to figure out if HR departments are trying to slot the applicant pool into a predictable range and only select those who will work for X dollars. Or have they been forced to do that by a higher authority? No matter the salary or hourly wage attached to a certain job, it seems fair and ethical to post it with the job duties and descriptions. To do otherwise is to force applicants into a guessing game where the end answer is almost always disappointing.

In many of the online applications I have seen, it's not possible for the applicant to put TBD (To Be Discussed) into the salary box, so this just leaves them in limbo. Consider that some people apply for management or supervisory positions in other cities or states. Do I want to drive to another town or another state only to be told that while I may have aced the interview the salary is nowhere near what I need to live on? You may say that pre-publishing the salary range for certain jobs is out of your control and just part of how Big HR does it in your city or county. But if you look at this issue as the number one complaint on LinkedIn by people applying for jobs, what can you do to change this practice at your library? You'll get happier, more enthusiastic, and more motivated applicants, eager to try and get the job if they know the pay and benefits in advance. The applicants who don't want to work for that salary range will self-select themselves out of the hiring process, thereby saving you time and effort. And it's just the ethical thing to do.

HIRING INTERVIEWS: IMPROVE THEM

If my review of LinkedIn (always a good collection of early-warning as to the do's and don'ts of the hiring process) is any indicator, here's a list of most applicants' major complaints:

- Salary not posted or discussed during the interview. (See above.)
- Benefits not described. (Do I get medical coverage for me and my spouse/ partner or not?)
- No response as to whether my submitted application or résumé was received or reviewed. (So common that it hardly needs mentioning, but I did, because it's polite, professional on our side, and important to the applicant.)
- Interviewer arrives late.
- Interviewer is not ready for the interview. (Hasn't reviewed the applicant's résumé; isn't familiar with the job the person is applying for.)
- Interviewer is distracted. (Takes phone calls, allows for staff interruptions, cuts the interview short to go and do something else or start another interview.)

- Interviewer doesn't take notes during the interview. (How will she or he remember who was who, among the collection of applicants?)
- Interviewer asks random, inappropriate, or illegal questions. (What year did you graduate high school?)
- No response back to the applicant—yea or nay—after the interview. (Ghosted.)
- The organization keeps posting the same job over and over again. (Meaning high turnover, mostly due to a toxic work culture or poor leadership.)

As an HR professional, your first set of responses to this Top Ten List of Interview Sins should be these: "I don't do any of those things as a skilled and prepared interviewer and more importantly, I don't let anyone who is hiring on behalf of our library engage in these unprofessional behaviors. We have a duty of care for our applicants. We should already have appropriate interview practices in place and continually develop our reputation for high standards during every stage of our hiring process. The interview is the gateway to the applicant's perception of our level of professionalism and the health of our work culture."

Of course, if you review LinkedIn for the most common complaints from hiring managers and HR people, it is this same list except it's flipped around on the applicant: late, unprepared, chews gum, dresses as if they're heading to the beach later, takes a call from their parents to ask how the interview is going, and so on.

THE POWER OF THE PANEL: INTERVIEW
APPROACHES FOR GROUP DECISIONS

Being a Bear of Small Brain, I really like to sit in as a member of an interview board. Much less pressure on me to make a "perfect hiring decision" (if that even exists) if I can watch the applicant engage with the group and then talk about his or her upsides and downsides when the coast is clear and they are no longer in the room.

The members of the panel interview team can be library leaders, managers, supervisors, or PICs from your library, other branches, and could even include library colleagues from other nearby library systems. You want a diversity of people on the panel, based on work experience, hiring knowledge, leadership skills, and other factors that create a fair and balanced group.

One tool that can help with the final interview decision, whether you're doing them alone and have to choose or you're part of or running a panel interview process, is your use or the group's use of the Forced Choice Matrix chart. There are several versions but the main point of the tool is to rank each applicant against each other until there is a clear winner. This works best when there are three to seven people going for the same position. (With two interviewees it's easy to choose; more than eight is tougher.)

The Matrix process says, "Who was the best candidate between Interviewee #1 and Interviewee #2?" This is based on their answers to our panel questions (which should be the same for each applicant), professional appearance, attitude, motivation to work, willingness to learn and be led, and so forth, through your collection of interviews, until it becomes clear that Interviewee #6 was the best-qualified person for the job, having been compared (forced choice means you have to pick one person over the other, for the tool to work correctly). It's possible that all of the panel members will have chosen #6 as well, which certainly makes the hiring process easier. It's possible that the majority in the room will have chosen #6, which means the others who did not can make their argument as to why they picked #3 or #7. If there is no general consensus among the panel—everyone picked someone different and feels strongly as to why, then you have to make some choices: Narrow the field from several to an agreed-upon few and do another round of interviews? Go back and take a longer look at the interview questions, to see if they match the job duties and job descriptions? Re-read the applicant's résumés again, to get more data? Keep voting until a clear choice is determined?

THE UNASKED TWO?

Here are two valuable and useful interview questions I almost never hear get asked during an in-person or panel interview process. Consider adding them to your list:

> Assume for a moment that you got this job. Tell people who know nothing about us what we do here.

> Assume for a moment that you got this job. Tell people who know nothing about us what you do here.

Both of these questions are valuable for several reasons:

The answers indicate that the applicant has done some of his or her own research about your library and the communities and patrons you serve.

It tells us the applicant has done more than just read your previously posted job duties and job descriptions and has even started to take a bit of ownership in your organization, by using work-inclusive pronouns like, "We do this . . ." and "I do that . . ." in her or his answers.

It suggests enthusiasm and motivation to do the job, because the person can already see herself or himself in that role.

Here's an example where things didn't go so well for two applicants who were applying for a member training job at a municipal insurance company. Their answers to each question left a lot to be desired:

Uh, you guys provide insurance to cities, covering a lot of different things.

Uh, I train people on how to understand their insurance coverages, I guess.

In the library world, what you want to hear an applicant answer for an entry-level library staff position is:

Well, I know this branch serves as the main location of the city or county library system. There are five other locations across the city or county, but this one is the hub of activity. We offer programs for toddlers and their parents, seniors, literacy programs for adults who need to learn to read, and we even have a free Legal Aid clinic here once a month, so people can clear up their court appearances. This branch has been here since 2011.

Does this (awesome) answer suggest that the applicant simply went on your website and memorized some facts? Yes, but not just that. The depth of this answer suggests this person has visited this branch (or others, what a concept!), perhaps has talked to other employees who work there or patrons who use the library, to get a sense of the place, and has done some additional computer work beyond just your library website, like going to your city/county's home page, or viewing a site from your library board or the Friends of the Library.

Onto the second question, again, for an entry-level library staff position:

Assume you already have the job. Tell us what you do here.

What you want to hear is: "I help people—all kinds of people in this community, of all ages—who come here. Some of them want a certain bestselling book and I can find it for them. Some want access to the Internet and I help them get online. Students come here from the junior high across the street to do homework. Some patrons just want a quiet place to read or study or do research, and I can help create that for them."

Is it possible the scope and depth of this person's answers here suggest she or he has worked in a library before? Certainly! But what if they have never worked in a library and yet these are their answers? I would have to hold myself back from leaping over the desk to shake their hand and welcome them aboard.

Compare and contrast these answers to both questions to the ones you may have already heard:

Question #1: "Uh, well, like it's the library, so you have a lot of books here and people can watch movies and go online for stuff. It's been here a long time and people come here to find what they're looking for."

Question #2: "Uh, well, I'm gonna be helping people check out books and I'll be putting books up on the shelves. You know, helping people who come in here find things. Keep the noisy kids quiet. Help the older folks. Go to meetings, listen to my boss tell me what to do."

Do the answers from the second applicant suggest someone who is just going through the motions to get through the interview, telling you what she or he thinks you want to hear, and faking it because they really don't know how the library functions, what role it plays in the community, and what library employees really do?

We can agree that for an entry-level library position that may be the person's first real job out of school, she or he doesn't have to have memorized the library's organizational leadership chart. But who would you prefer to hire, someone who has done the required research and wants the job, or someone who hasn't and kinda, sorta doesn't really want the job?

We will certainly have higher hiring standards and different expectations for the interview of a library leader, department manager, or supervisor, but those two questions work pretty well at those levels too. Is the applicant able to demonstrate why she or he is the right person for that job, at any level?

Perhaps this all goes back to the difference between hiring someone with lots of experience and not much enthusiasm for the job, versus hiring someone with no or limited experience and what seems like genuine enthusiasm. All things being equal, if you've worked in HR, can you say from what you have witnessed that we can teach technical skills but we can't teach employees to like their jobs, like serving their patrons, and like working with their colleagues?

An HR colleague tells her own story: "My husband and I were looking to hire a babysitter for our three kids. The first teenager told us she had lots of babysitting experience but didn't seem to want the job that much. The second teenager said she didn't have much babysitting experience but she had taken a Child Development class at school and just got her infant/child/adult CPR certification from the local Red Cross. She seemed like she really wanted the job, plus she had done some things to improve on her lack of experience, so we hired her."

HR life is not that easy, but the model makes sense to me.

THE CLUB SANDWICH/SOCIAL INTERVIEW

There are many versions of this interview approach, some of them may
be apocryphal (or made up, because it sounds fun to talk about the scene),
and some may have happened. The Social Interview is most often used for
applicants who are taking on a leadership, management, or key supervisory
role, where they will have a goodly number of people working for them and
it's especially important to make certain there is a good fit with the potential
staffers. If we in HR agree that great people skills are equally as important
as great technical skills (and on my measurement scale, even more critical
for managerial success), then hiring for fit means we may need to think
outside the box as we narrow our choice of an applicant. Hence the Social
Interview, which can take place at a coffee shop or a restaurant out in the
real world, or even at a makeshift potluck meal or catered staff lunch at the
library.

The approach is always the same: as we get down to our final one or two
or three applicants, let's get each one, alone, into a social situation and watch
how he or she engages with staff in the break room, or in the coffee/restaurant
situation, in public with the barista or a waiter/waitress. How does this person
treat the coffee counter staff? How does this person engage with a waiter or
waitress, especially when there is an error in the food delivery process?

Are they polite, meek, dismissive, rude, sarcastic?

Here's the version I heard from a CEO, back in my early coaching days:

> I always take the final applicant to lunch at my favorite restaurant. It's a casual
> dining spot and the food is good and the service even better. I clear it with my
> waiter/waitress in advance that no matter what the applicant orders, bring him
> or her an iced tea and a club sandwich. If they actually order an iced tea and a
> club sandwich, then switch up their drink and food with something else. I want
> to see how this person reacts.

From this CEO's point of view, if the applicant eats the club sandwich and
drinks the iced tea without saying anything, she or he may be too hesitant,
not confident in her or his initial decision, or not willing to make changes in
the work environment. If the applicant berates the waiter/waitress and says,
"You messed up my order!" in a rude or condescending way, then that's a red
flag about his or her future behavior, especially when it comes to supervising others. The perfect response, of course, is, "Hi, I actually ordered a club
sandwich and a diet soda. Can I send these both back with you? No worries,
you can bring his food and I'll wait for mine. Thanks."

Is this a foolproof way to assess an applicant's people skills? It seems a
little childish, but I'll let you be the judge.

A few thoughts: Do people really have or show "two behaviors"? The one they want their potential bosses or future co-workers to see, versus their real behavior? The social interview technique is one that might best be used for applicants in high-level library leadership positions, especially for those that require a lot of community interactions, public meetings, board responsibilities, and media face time.

Just be ready for it if you're applying for a job and you get a club sandwich delivered to your table.

CHECK YOUR HIRING BIASES AT THE OFFICE DOOR

There is much discussion in the media and the workplace about Diversity, Equity, and Inclusion, or DEI. It describes a collection of sought-after behaviors that provide for fairness in our hiring processes, supervision, and promotion of all employees. It seeks to provide equal opportunities and support for employees in what are called "protected classes." Most of us are in at least one: age (over forty); race; country of origin; gender; gender identity, sexual orientation; transgender identity; domestic violence victimhood; veterans' status; religious or political beliefs; physical or psychological disabilities; health conditions; and pregnancy, just to name a few. DEI training programs seek to build awareness about past discriminatory practices, level the playing field of employment and promotion, and increase the creativity, problem-solving, and success of the organization, by bringing in different people who offer different viewpoints.

Part of the DEI training discussion includes the realities of our biases, the assumptions we make about each other, often based on sweeping generalizations or a negative encounter with someone, who certainly does not represent the larger population of that particular group. These biases often come from our environment, our exposure to what we are told to think about people different from us by our parents, family, friends, school interactions, or workplaces. They are often defined as "confirmation biases," where our negative encounters with people in any of the protected classes lead us to generalize and thereby confirm, "That's how those people are." We all have our biases and part of DEI awareness building is to change our thinking about how we perceive others. This takes effort, but the resulting changes in our perceptions can lead us to a better understanding, fairer treatment, patience, empathy, and acceptance.

We know that biases exist in our personal and professional lives. It has been illegal for many decades for companies to use biases to discriminate against people during hiring, and how they are supervised or promoted. It's unethical and can subject an organization to a civil suit. The problem with bias is that it can be subtle. When it's about skin color or gender, it's obviously wrong; when it's about bias connected to *perceptions of performance*, it can be nearly as harmful but less obvious. Consider if you have seen or experienced (or worse, used) any of these forms of *perceptional bias*:

Age bias: "This employee is too old or too young to do this new type of library work or to figure out this complex technical equipment, or process this type of information in our ever-changing library workspace. He or she is too old to learn new things or too young to know how to operate the way we do here or to figure it out." The assumption here is that this is a permanent condition, and that they won't be able to learn anything new.

Experience bias: "This employee lacks the life or work experience to do what we are asking. He or she hasn't done this job or this type of work and doesn't have the technical expertise to work in our library, know-how, or 'time in grade.'" The assumption here is because they haven't done it before elsewhere, even at a branch in another city or state, they won't have the capacity to learn it here.

Motivation bias: "This employee doesn't seem to care. He or she is kind of a loner, doesn't jump into group projects, has a 'lousy attitude,' seems to be standoffish, and doesn't seem to want to take on new challenges, or mix with other library staff." This assumption may not take into consideration that this employee is introverted, prefers to work alone, and may even be burned out because he or she has not been praised, supported, challenged, heard, or fairly managed.

Success bias: What we predict about an employee's success in the organization often occurs because we manage him or her to that expectation. "He's probably not going to do very well" comes true, as does, "She's going to do very well here." This bias comes because of a preconceived notion of predicted success. Some library managers and supervisors can make this one come true by what they do or don't do for their employees, right at the start. This certainly points to why a skillful onboarding and new-employee orientation process is so critical at the start of the library staffer's career.

Recognizing workplace biases is half the issue. The other half requires a commitment to see they are eliminated and that we hire, promote, and manage all employees fairly, ethically, and equally. The adage, "Don't judge a book by its cover," means we should stop perception bias, set high performance and behavioral standards, provide opportunities for all employees to prove themselves, and coach them toward a level of success that satisfies them and the organization.

EXIT INTERVIEWS: DO THEM AND USE THE
INFORMATION GOING FORWARD

I'm a firm believer in the value and necessity of an exit interview for every employee who leaves your library voluntarily. I'll grant that we probably don't need to do one for the furious employee who flings his or her ID badge at you, like the late great magician Ricky Jay hurling a sharpened playing card into a watermelon, but for those employees who are quitting on a mostly cooperative level, their comments as to why are valuable. If one employee tells you why he or she is leaving and it doesn't have anything to do with policy violations, patron behavioral issues, or conflicts with co-workers, wish him or her well on their occupational journey. But several employees who leave for the same reasons listed in the previous sentence should be a big warning light to you to investigate the overall management approach, the supervisory styles of certain bosses, and the level of toxicity in the work culture.

The fact that the exit interview should be done by an HR representative, not the employee's manager or supervisor or the library director, should be a given. Few employees will have the desire to tell the real truth to their soon-to-be former boss, as to why they are leaving, especially since we can often correctly guess that the primary reason was how they were treated and supervised by that boss. Here are two examples:

HR: "Can I ask you why you are leaving our library?"

EE: "I don't feel I have been given a fair opportunity to advance my career."

HR: "How so?"

EE: "Well, my boss never seemed to give me any guidance about how to promote to the next level. I saw her talking with other co-workers about going back to school and taking some technical classes, but I never heard that from her."

HR: "I'm sorry to hear you felt like you weren't informed about those possibilities. Did you ever have any one-on-one conversations with your manager, like coaching conversations, where she asked you about your career goals at the library?"

EE: "Not that I remember."

This example points to a possible disconnect between the employee and her boss. Those coaching conversations may have happened with the employee and they may not have. Following the exit interview, part of your HR role is to have a candid conversation with the departing employee's boss to get her side. Perhaps she will admit that she didn't reach out to the employee with enough specific guidance, which should be part of her new approach with all of her staff going forward. Or maybe she did explain the opportunities for promotion, over a series of coaching conversations, which she documented, and can show you.

Here's a more challenging exit interview example:

HR: "Can I ask you why you are leaving our library?"

EE: "Well, I'm being harassed by a patron."

HR: "Really? Who?"

EE: "That guy that always comes in on Wednesday nights, wearing the puffy jacket and the backward hat. He was always saying rude things about my body and trying to hug me."

HR: "Wow. When did this start?"

EE: "About six months ago."

HR: "What? Why didn't you tell your boss, or me, or the director? We would have addressed that immediately and banned him either temporarily or permanently."

EE: (one of four or more possible answers) "I didn't think you'd believe me. I didn't think you would be able to do anything about it. I didn't think you would do anything about it. I didn't know who to tell."

This scenario illustrates two problems: Some employees may not believe the organization will do anything to stop harassment aimed at them by patrons or worse, by bosses, and it points to a work culture issue that creates obstacles to this being reported, by both the targeted employee and by the bystander-employees, who have certainly seen or heard about this harassment.

There are some less-forward thinking HR types who might conduct an exit interview like this and think, "Well, it's too late for me to do anything about this now. The employee is already out the door." Wrong response.

True HR professionals would say to the departing employee: "I'm sorry to hear this happened to you and I'm even more sorry to hear you either didn't know about our reporting process or didn't trust our response to your concern. I'm telling you now I will investigate this issue as soon as we are done here and I will get back in contact with you by phone or email to tell you what we have done to prevent this from happening to another employee. You will hear from me soon on this and I will tell you what actions we will take."

Perhaps that employee goes away and thinks you'll never get back in touch. But more importantly, when you do follow up with this employee with an informative, concluding email or written letter, it proves you keep your promises and that your organization takes these concerns seriously and enforces consequences when they believe them to be true, even if the employee is no longer working for you.

Chapter 2

The Hiring Process

Recruiting, Job Duties and Descriptions, Screening, and Selections

One of my favorite quotes about the working life comes from management guru Warren Bennis:

> The factory of the future will have only two employees, a man and a dog. The man will be there to feed the dog. The dog will be there to keep the man from touching the equipment.[1]

Besides having seven dogs myself (because eight would be too many and six would not been enough), his quote is indicative of the potential issues HR professionals face as we navigate through Artificial Intelligence (AI); robots in the workplace beyond just the factory floor (meaning some even might be installed as bosses); permanent WFH (where we never physically see employees, who are working for us from Europe, Asia, Africa, or Antarctica); and the constant evolution of tech as a way to replace the seemingly now-quaint application of human elbow grease to a problem, opportunity, deadline, or project.

WANT MORE JOB APPLICANTS? BE PREPARED TO OFFER MORE

For lots of reasons—psychological, economic, political, and pandemic—the labor pool is not sufficient for many jobs in the current market. Service industry jobs in particular have gone unfilled, with stories on the Internet of restaurants offering $25 per hour for dishwashers. Many longtime restaurants, retail stores, and service businesses have closed, partly because the owners could not get any qualified help. We appear to be in a perfect storm, created by job dissatisfaction in general and the demand for higher pay for jobs that have been considered as low-skill/high turnover.

It's common here locally and across the country to see "Help Wanted" signs posted in the windows of convenience stores, restaurants, and retail shops. Auto dealers need both salespeople and mechanics. The healthcare profession continues to need more physicians, nurses, and support staff. Factories, trucking, and manufacturing companies are always posting billboards looking for applicants for well-paying jobs, with full healthcare benefits. Calling the 800 numbers for large service companies gives us some version of this now-usual complaint: "Due to unusually high call volumes, we are experiencing unfortunate delays and may be unable to complete your call promptly." In other words, "We Don't Have Enough Staff."

Applicants with certain in-demand skills in many fields that are going begging can do something only professional athletes do—negotiate their salary, benefits, and extra compensation. If you need to hire, and soon, you may have to do likewise, using the lure of higher-than-normal salaries and more employee benefits than usual. It is a sign of our times that many applicants now control more of their fate than ever before. If that is so, consider these general hiring criteria:

Don't sacrifice employee quality for employee quantity. Just because you need people, don't skip critical steps like full interviews, application and résumé screenings, and background checks. Better to wait for the best applicant to apply—Ms. or Mr. Right, not just Ms. or Mr. Right Now.

Reward your current employees with bonuses for bringing good new hires to you. Your current employees can help you find talented people, if the rewards for doing so are in place. As long as the referral process is fair to all applicants, give more than just verbal or written praise to employees who bring you their qualified (or at the least, motivated) friends or colleagues who might be a good fit and want a career in the library services world. Gift cards, a discretionary day off, or a cash bonus can be an enticing incentive for your staff to be on the lookout for potential new hires.

Beef up your training, onboarding, and new-employee orientation processes. I'll discuss this in more detail in the next chapter. New jobs can be overwhelming and new hires who are not supported during that critical first day, first week, and first month may leave for a job where the pay might not be better but the work culture is.

Post the salary range in your job postings. A review of most LinkedIn postings by job seekers shows that this is one of the main complaints of many applicants: "Don't leave out this important information that helps me decide if your company is right for me. If I go through an interview, only to find out at the end of the discussion that the job doesn't pay enough, we have wasted each other's time." Salaries are rarely a secret in government jobs; they are already posted online by the media, public watchdog groups, and recruiters. Be honest about your pay practices and tell applicants up front.

Provide for work-life balance. The need for employees can mean that those already on the job are being worked down to the nub. Overtime is great for the wallet and bad for the physical and mental health of employees. Don't burn out your longtime employees and force them into seeking other less stressful positions, and don't overwhelm your new hires into wanting to leave because of a grueling work pace. If you can continue to offer remote work options, do so. Getting work done is only possible when you have people to do it.

BENCHMARKING SALARIES WITH FORMAL SURVEYS AND JOB CLASSIFICATION STUDIES

Studying pay scales for the libraries in your city, county, or state sounds less than glamorous but it's necessary and done correctly, provides useful data as to how to position your library for more successful hires. There can be a tendency in HR to rely on outdated data, to compare your library to another in a community where the socioeconomic levels are completely different, or worse, to not measure salaries because it becomes one of those "when we can get around to it" projects.

Benchmarking your library is really a two-part process: we look at the job duties and descriptions for all the salaried and hourly positions in our building, district, collection of branches, and then we compare our rates of pay to the most comparable geographic areas, the size of our employee population, and the size of our communities served. We're attempting to keep the playing field level, so that when we make business decisions about changing or updating job duties and job descriptions and the pay for them—usually approved by the library director, in conjunction with the library board, or city council/county board of supervisors' agreement and support—it's based on real, verified, and current data.

In my experience, it's harder to do the former—update job duties and job descriptions—than the latter, assess pay scales. We can discover what other libraries pay their personnel; the challenge comes in fine-tuning the language for job duties and descriptions, especially in libraries with unions or employee associations, which want a heavy say in what is finally agreed upon for their members.

I have seen antiquated job duties—"must be able to lift 50 pounds overhead," "type 65 words per minute," or "be fluent in Microsoft Office"—that don't match the current library jobs. Job classification studies require finesse and careful wording. Some library HR departments start by asking all of the employees to self-assess: "Tell us exactly what you do here, by listing every single one of your daily tasks, in detail."

Of course, this can cause a near-mutiny among the employees, as they either try to overload HR with six pages of "and then I do this, and then I do that" or they simply don't participate in the process. "You figure it out" is the response from those who don't want management to get any ideas about making their jobs more difficult, time intensive, or tedious.

There are two ways most HR departments conduct these benchmarking/survey projects, which often take longer than first expected to complete. One approach is to have your most qualified HR staff member(s) do it, who has the experience, head for numbers, and ability to do the necessary deep research. The other approach is to hire it out, using qualified HR consultants who do this work regularly and have all the necessary tools and research processes to provide you with complete reports in both areas.

Hiring this work out is not cheap, but it's often faster than your own HR shop could do it and probably more accurate. (It's like the difference between selling your house yourself or hiring a realtor. You could probably do it, but they know how already, usually way better than you.) Get several estimates from consulting firms, look at the quality of their sample reports, and choose the best for your library's size and employee population.

SCREENING FOR HIRING

This sounds like HR heresy, but can we go back to having people look at the paper products people have created, with an eye toward selecting them into the organization rather than screening them out? I fully realize if you have fifty applicants for a library leadership position (and you are fully blessed if you get that many), you will have to spend hours looking through paper applications and résumés to size them up for a possible interview.

But paper résumés and paper applications can tell us a lot. Neatness counts, so does accuracy, and missing or questionable information can leap out at us, which the software screening might miss. I don't trust the HR software because it's sterile. Holding an applicant's résumé or application in my hand gives me a lot of information that I can assess. Scrawled with a crayon, ink stains all over it? Odd paper color and strange font? A photo of the applicant on the résumé? (This is a new effort by young job hunters to stand out from the crowd by being memorable. Photos on résumés usually get tossed immediately because no hiring organization wants to be accused later of only hiring "pretty people," young people, or by-passing qualified diversity applicants.)

Since we work in Human Resources, I'd like for us to break the habit of relying solely on machines to do the screening and selection work humans used to do. Gone are the days, it appears, when HR assistants, analysts, managers, and directors actually looked at paper résumés, let alone an actual job application. The machines have become self-aware. Today, it seems our "best" applicants have figured out how to game the HRIS system by tricking the scanning software into pulling their résumés and applications out of the electronic pile. But that doesn't mean they are the most qualified or even the most enthusiastic applicants; it just means they are more skilled at adding in keywords and manipulating the selection process.

LET'S TALK ABOUT REFERENCE CHECKS

In my perfect library HR world, let's say we have a collection of applicants who have made it through our initial pre-screening steps (they have the work experience, education, or certifications we have deemed useful for that particular job). Once they are on our list of initial interviews, I would call their previous employers and say, "Can we email you over a signed waiver from the applicant, and once you have it, ask you to answer these questions?"

- Dates of hire and leaving?
- Job title and job duties?
- Salary or hourly pay rate?
- Since we have provided a signed release of liability waiver from the applicant, could we get a copy of the person's last performance evaluation? (It's rare that they will agree to it, but it never hurts to ask.)
- Would you rehire this person? If not, can you say why? Did they leave amicably, with notice, or get fired? (Again, not usually information they will easily tell you, but at least you can demonstrate some due diligence by asking. Remind them this question may be part of a box that was checked during their exit interview.)

Two bonus questions: Did this person engage in any racially or sexually harassing behaviors while working for you? Did this person engage in any criminal or ethical acts that violated the law or your policies?

In my experience, HR departments are too shy about asking tough questions about the applicant's work history. Hiring people is expensive, time-consuming, and fraught with legal peril if it's done wrong. Can we at least say we made a valiant effort to determine if this person is a good fit in our library? If we believe, as I do, that past work behavior is a decent (and imperfect) predictor of future work behavior, then we owe it to our organization to screen correctly, legally, and diligently.

I like job applications with three professional references where the applicant used to work, so we can do something too many HR people skip: call and verify employment dates, job duties, or any other information the previous employer feels they want to give us. To get this look into their past, we must have a signed waiver from the applicant that says, as part of our next-steps background checks, they will allow us to contact previous employers. Too many HR departments skip the professional reference check process because they say, "No past employer will tell us anything useful. They might verify employment dates but that's about it."

What if none of the applicant's previous employers answer any questions about him or her, even when given a signed waiver? Will they answer the question of whether he or she would be eligible to be rehired by them? Not a good sign if there is only complete silence from everywhere this person worked.

What about checking the applicant's personal references? I would put this into the "Complete Waste of Time" category because the information we receive is tainted by the applicant's relationship with the reference. Would you ever include a personal reference who would not say all positive things about you to a hiring entity? Of course not. Do you expect the people provided by the applicant to say, "Lies, Cheats, Steals, Harasses, Lazy" or "Barely gets feet wet when walks upon the water"?

However, I do consider it to be a red flag warning if you do call all of the applicant's personal references and either don't get any calls back or the numbers are mysteriously disconnected. This goes double for calling the applicant's previous employers. If they are all "closed and went out of business" that arouses suspicion.

I believe our hiring approach should be, "Prove to us why we should hire you. We will never be desperate enough to hire someone without going through a structured, legal, vetting process. We will not take shortcuts when it comes to placing someone into our organization who could cause harm to our employees, patrons, facility, collections, or reputation in the community. We have an expectation that all employees will work hard, serve our patrons, and each other, and get along while doing so. As such, we will be choosy as to who we hire. We would rather say no at the application stage than to have to fire this person or worse, see her or him in a civil court, because it was not a good fit from the start."

BACKGROUND CHECKS

Do them. Okay, moving on.

I have testified in several expert witness civil cases where the HR issue I focused on was, "Why didn't you do a background check on this person? He turned out later to be a major crook and now you are paying dearly for it." Your defense of "He looked like a decent guy" or "It's too expensive to do a background check on everyone" doesn't work for a jury.

It's certainly true that we all get a vibe from applicants during interviews. Relying solely on your intuition is both unfair and unethical. You can't judge a book by its cover (even inside the library). What your gut feels about an applicant can be far from reality, which is why background checks are so revealing.

I'm reminded of an HR colleague who told me she was once recruiting for a chief of police for her city. The final step in the selection process was a polygraph examination. (These are used commonly in law enforcement hirings.) The applicant they had pre-selected passed all their requirements easily and failed the polygraph (twice) due to his unethical behaviors at his former agency. He had tried to talk her out of making him take the polygraph, claiming it was unnecessary, but she held firm and he didn't get the position.

When I offer my clients hiring advice I often say, "First, find a skilled background check provider, with a well-established national reputation, and who understands the legal complexities involved. Have them provide you with the necessary waiver forms to give to the applicant. Make certain they can demonstrate to you they have a full understanding of the Fair Credit Reporting Act, which requires we provide all applicants a full copy of their background check report, with an opportunity to refute any errors."

"Second," I say, "have your library attorney review all of the forms and procedures used by the background check firm you choose."

"Third, don't skip steps or make value judgments based on appearance. Use these procedures for every position, even part-time or even volunteer ones."

"Fourth, don't ever solely rely on an 'intuitive feel' about an applicant. Lots of skilled and smart people have been fooled by an applicant who shined in an interview, which made them skip the background check because she or he 'seemed like a great person,' only to have this person cause the whole organization tremendous pain later on."

While every position in the library should require a background check, certain ones need even more scrutiny, including jobs where the applicant will:

- Have cash-handling or fiduciary responsibilities.
- Work with children or the elderly on an unsupervised basis.
- Perform a security function in the library.

BACKGROUND CHECK OBSTACLES

I always suggest that every background check include a civil index check, where the search firm provides a history of any litigation the applicant has been involved in, as either a defendant or a plaintiff. To get this data, the investigating firm will have to research every county where this person has lived. This can be a bit more expensive but in my experience, it's always worth it.

This includes civil suits based on employment issues (wrongful terminations, harassment claims, workers' compensation claims); restraining orders (either as the restrained party or the person requesting the order); lawsuits against cities or counties for frivolous reasons; and slip and fall or auto accident litigation. Has this person been labeled as a "vexatious litigant" by the courts—meaning he or she has filed so many useless lawsuits, most often representing themselves "pro per" or "pro se" without an attorney—so that the courts no longer allow them to file another one?

I recall meeting with an attorney to provide expert witness help. He had been sued by his former legal assistant for sexual harassment. There was no validity to her case, and it was further confirmed that she had sued three other law firms, making the same harassment claims each time. A civil index check would have spotted these suits and she never would have been hired, at least by my client's firm.

I'm not saying don't hire an applicant who has had contact with the criminal or civil courts process, only that you look at the context of that involvement and make a fair, legal, and ethical business decision based on the type of job and the person's history. I would hire an applicant for my library who had admitted that she or he filed for bankruptcy, just not to be the finance manager.

What will you do if the applicant's background check reveals he is on your state's Sex Offender Database? (The list is filled almost entirely by convicted males.) It's also known as the "Megan's Law" database, which is accessible online, by anyone, in all fifty states. (Don't read the history of how this law came to pass if you are triggered by disturbing sex crime descriptions.)

The information below is from the California Megan's Law website (https://www.meganslaw.ca.gov/About_Penalties.aspx):

A person is authorized to use information disclosed on this website only to protect a person at risk. *Except to protect a person at risk* [emphasis mine] or as authorized under any other law, use of any information disclosed on this website for purposes relating to any of the following is prohibited:

- Health insurance
- Insurance
- Loans
- Credit
- Employment
- Education, scholarships, or fellowships
- Housing or accommodations
- Benefits, privileges, or services provided by any business establishment

Most states require or authorize the following types of businesses to evaluate sex offender registry information in their hiring processes:

- K–12 schools
- Daycares and preschools
- Humane societies
- Government agencies
- Adoption agencies
- Public housing authorities
- Financial institutions
- In-home care agencies

You should review the law in your state to determine whether your library falls under an exempted category. As a library, you might also meet an exception for employers to use sex offender registry information to protect at-risk people. If this exception applies in your state, your organization will likely qualify if your employees work with children, disabled people, or the elderly. I'm not a lawyer, but I would argue to you (and your labor law lawyer) that you can make the argument that as a "government agency" that has "employees who work with children, disabled people, and the elderly," you can not hire applicants who are on your state's Sex Offender database.

Does your state have what is now called "Ban the Box" legislation in place that prevents deep-dive criminal background checks or using someone's long-past conviction history as a barrier to employment? Stay legal with this concern and follow your state's specific guidelines of what you can and can't ask on your applications, during the interview, and as part of the background screening process.

When it comes to hiring people with an admitted or discovered criminal conviction, every organization should weigh three critical issues, as suggested by the US Equal Employment Opportunity Commission (EEOC):

- the nature and seriousness of the offense/crime;
- the time that has passed since the criminal offense or completion of the sentence (no more than seven years ago is the usual criteria for how long is long enough to look back into the person's criminal past);
- and the nature of the job.

Part of the national movement to "Ban the Box" on criminal convictions is to help people who have been incarcerated get a second chance at a job and not continue to punish them once they have moved through the criminal justice system. The presence of a criminal conviction is not an automatic disqualification for a job in your library. Use the EEOC's three-part criteria as you make your decision. If you need more clarification and guidance on specific applicants, contact your library's labor law attorney and explain the job and your concerns.

THE PROBATIONARY PERIOD

It's easy to forget that the probationary period for an employee at your library is a two-way decision point. It certainly gives HR, the employee's supervisor(s), and his or her co-workers a chance to assess their overall fit for the job, taking in job skills, initiative, and positive interactions with patrons and colleagues, all important to note. The period can range from ninety days (probably a tad too short for my liking), to six months (my preferred span), to one year (probably too long, unless the job is complex, strategic, or a high-level leadership position). We use these periods to assess the new employee's current and potential abilities: Has he or she learned on the job? Will he or she continue to learn on the job, to master the necessary skills well before or at least by the end of the period? And does he or she demonstrate the best balance of technical skills, job knowledge, know his or her job duties, complete quality work, meet deadlines, keep promises, and have the interpersonal skills that we all want to be around?

On occasion, I will hear an HR manager or HR analyst lament, "We should have gotten rid of that employee long before his or her probationary period was up, because now, thanks to our civil service rules or union/employee association MOUs, it's practically impossible to fire him or her."

When I inquire further, I usually hear some version of a story that suggests they waited for that person to improve their people skills, not his or her technical skills. And the tale of HR woe will have an "if only" variation to it, as in, "If only her interactions with patrons were as good as her computer skills. She's our best IT person but the patrons on the library floor—and her co-workers who call her at the Help Desk—can't stand her lousy attitude."

This falls into the "Let's hope she gets nicer over time" category, where we want her to improve her people skills and give her enough time to do so, but it doesn't happen. We then miss the opportunity to jettison her before the probationary period, often because of guilt, not wanting to have the Necessary Hard Conversation, or simply not realizing the decision deadline is approaching. (This last should further exemplify the need for careful HRIS and records management systems.)

Let's go back to the two-way street decision point. At any point during the probationary period, the employee can decide to leave as well. He or she says, "This is not the job for me or not what I thought it was going to be," and quits, sometimes giving advanced notice, sometimes not showing up ever again, or just walking out the door, mid-shift, for the last time.

All this leads me to Albrecht's Law: "Bad in the beginning, bad in the middle, means it's going to be bad in the end." I have proved this personally with blind first dates, initial client discussions, and dinner parties. What starts out poorly rarely gets way better and it often gets worse. (I'll dive into the value of probationary periods even more in chapter 6 on discipline.)

Feeling miserable about an employee who makes others miserable can lead us to variations of these horrible and wrong conclusions: "We can't fire anyone around here, without a letter from the President of the United States. It takes an act of Congress to get rid of someone around here. If we tried to fire him at this late date, we're just setting ourselves up to get sued." The real answers to those howling laments should be, "No, no, and not necessarily."

In the next chapter, I'll discuss the value of the onboarding and orientation processes for new employees, to help them start and stay at your library.

NOTE

1. Eigen, Lewis D. and Jonathan P. Siegel. (1989). *The Manager's Book of Quotations*. AMACOM.

Chapter 3

Onboarding and Training New Hires

Setting Them Up for Continued Success

The onboarding process strikes me as such a fragile time. Think back to every job you've ever had and how poorly or how well your bosses back then (or the HR Department, if the company was big enough) covered all the information you needed to know as you began. While it was certainly important for you to know how to fill out your time card, was it not more important to feel welcomed, included in the work culture immediately, and supported in those first critical days and weeks? My experience is that the list of private sector companies and public sector agencies that do this well is shorter than the list of those who don't. We don't toss toddlers or anyone else who doesn't know how to swim into the deep end of a pool and hope they figure it out before they drown. It seems some organizations have an attitude that says, "Well, into the water you go! Sink or swim!"

As both an exercise in nostalgia and an assessment of the amount and quality of the support you received, take twenty minutes and make a list of every job you've ever held, from high school forward to now.

Consider the new-employee orientation process for each as: None, Fair, Acceptable, and Outstanding. This can include the training you received, any shadowing of an employee who was either kind enough or grudgingly had to show you the ropes, as it were, or classroom/formal group meeting orientation sessions. This may have taken place in one hour, over one day, or for several weeks, depending on the complexity of the job and the amount of formal structure to their onboarding process.

Here's my list of every job and the measurement of the quality of the support, training, and orientation I received at the outset:

- Dishwasher at a buffet restaurant; age fifteen: None (I was so naive, I didn't think I could take a bathroom break for the first three months I worked there).
- Grocery store employee; six years, during high school and college: Acceptable.

Side jobs, while working at the grocery store, in college:

- Sold clothes at a store, similar to The Gap or American Eagle: Fair.
- Bouncer/Security Guard at high school and college football games, concerts: None.
- Telemarketing for software sales: Outstanding (full disclosure—my dad's company).
- Ramp Agent/Baggage Handler for an airline: Fair (they sent me to a week-long school, but none of the equipment they trained us on matched what they used at my airport).
- Staff writer, catalog company for books and training materials: Outstanding (okay, so I went back to my dad's company for a bit after college).
- City of San Diego employee, for ten years: Outstanding.
- City of San Diego supervisor, for five years: Outstanding.
- Consultant, Author, Trainer, Speaker: Lots of advice and support from colleagues in similar careers, but I learned mostly on the job and via the school of hard knocks.

Let's do the math: ten paid jobs in my life, so removing my current gig and the two times my dad paved my way, the seven remaining hardly paint a glowing or perfect portrait of early support for long-term success. None (2), Fair (2), Acceptable (1), Outstanding (2). Here's a not-so-shocking conclusion: I did not last too long at the Nones and the Fairs. I stayed six years at the Acceptable (grocery store) and fifteen years at the Outstanding (City of San Diego).

Is your list better or worse than mine? Did you quit those jobs, where you got no initial support, within the first week (or even on or just after the first day?), or within a few months? It's hard to make it a year—to get beyond the probation period some organizations have—if you are miserable, unfulfilled, mistreated, or ignored every working day. Those employees who feel unsupported by their bosses and not connected (or even covertly or overtly shunned) by their co-workers soon develop a "vision ailment"; it's not an "Eye Problem" but an "I Problem." They start saying, "I can't come in today. I'm going to call in sick. I don't like it there. I don't feel connected. I hate this place. I either don't like my boss, my co-workers, or the customers, or worse, all three. I need to look for another job. I'm going to quit."

If we could activate the Feel-Better Time Machine for this employee, what would we do differently to make her or him feel informed, connected, and appreciated?

THE "ONBOARDING CEREMONY": FORMAL VERSUS INFORMAL ORIENTATION

The first day of a new job, like the first day of school—at any grade level, including college—is a stressful moment for even the most calm and collected employee. Even people who have had a long working career feel anxious walking into a new building, meeting an avalanche of new people, and trying to determine what will be expected of them.

Consider the possibility that working for your library might be an employee's first "real job." They may be just out of high school, fresh from a few years of college, a new graduate, or even a person who is returning to the workforce after a long hiatus (going back to work after their kids have grown and moved out, after a divorce or the death of a spouse or partner, moving to a new city and starting a fresh job anew). And like the first day of school, first impressions matter. We want to impress upon new employees that this library will be a place they can stay and be well-treated, rewarded, protected, and given the chance to learn, advance, or promote, for as long as they choose to stay there.

Based on their need for information, our orientation process is going to be different for new library directors, deputy directors, and department heads, than it will be for managers, first-line supervisors, and PICs. New frontline staff, including part-time employees and even volunteers, will have different needs, and will first want to see where and how they will fit in. This makes orientations at every level different in some respects, similar in others, but should be customized to fit the nature of the person's job title, duties, and responsibilities.

Depending on the size of the organization and the number of new employees coming in, the orientation process can range from casual to formal. While longer isn't necessarily better, what doesn't work is the hour-long "briefing" by an HR representative and a quick tour of the facility: "Here's your cubicle. There's the bathroom. The break room is down the hall. Your boss will show you how to fill out your time card using our software system. Let me know if you have any questions. Good luck and thanks for coming!"

This is potentially an anxious time for new employees. The orientation process either creates a success model for them to follow or it can make them feel alienated. As the HR professional, you may be the first "real" representative of the library that these employees see. Your initial welcome—based on a solid and well-designed orientation program—should serve to answer their questions, lessen their anxieties, give them a chance to hear from the leaders, and meet their soon-to-be daily colleagues. A strong orientation program can give them a sense of inclusion and confidence that will get them all started on the right path.

Here are some of the value-added reasons why we want to conduct new-hire orientation programs:

- To provide an early, positive view of the organization, by being inclusive and welcoming of them.
- To let them know what will be expected from them, in terms of attendance, job performance, work behavior, cooperation, and service to the patrons, co-workers, and leaders.
- To help them understand professional boundaries, their responsibilities to not engage in harassment and report it if they witness it or it happens to them, and to follow our HR rules and policies.
- To have us teach them the "real rules of success" and not learn them from their co-workers (who may not know them either).
- To help them know we are here to help them complete their probationary periods successfully.
- To help them absorb the library culture and assimilate quickly.
- To build their morale at an early stage.
- To give them the availability and access to the people and the resources to help them succeed.
- To give them a chance to succeed, on fair, equitable, ethical, and legal grounds, with their co-workers.
- To build a sense of connection, cohesion, and stability, so they can be productive, comfortable, and confident, as soon as they can.

ONBOARDING SUBJECTS

This is your list of topics to cover, both during informal meetings, formal training classes or small-group discussions, one-on-one conversations, or "walk and talks," where HR or a manager or a supervisor takes one or a group of new employees throughout the facility, explaining, demonstrating, and helping them meet and greet their new colleagues. ("Over here, we have our two-story break room, which has a coffee shop with seventeen baristas, a fitness center, and a day spa.")

Consider how you will add to and modify this list of first-day, first-week tasks, based on your library's work culture, its position in the community (rural, urban, suburban, small branch, large main branch/HQ, etc.), and the nature of the person's job.

- Our Employee Manual or Our Library Policies and Procedures Manual. (If it's a longer, more complete version of the Employee Manual.) Sample discussion: "You can find full and complete descriptions of these policies and procedures on our Intranet site or in this full version of the P&P Manual, which you have just been given. Please speak to your supervisor or call HR if you have questions or concerns about the language of any of our policies. You are fully responsible for following them, even if we don't cover them today."
- The library's overall mission statement, the organizational chart, and the mission statement for each department.
- HR-related forms: I-9 forms; Social Security forms; employee contact information; W-9 forms; probationary periods; Americans with Disabilities Act (ADA) and Family Medical Leave Act (FMLA) accommodations; sick leave, time off, and vacation policies; discipline policies.
- Union or employee association rules and/or Memos of Understanding (MOUs); union representative contact information.
- Pay and benefits forms and procedures: how to get paid, legally and accurately, using time cards and/or our software.
- The Library's Code of Patron Conduct.
- IT Procedures: safe Internet and Intranet use; setting up email accounts and passwords; protecting our data and devices.
- Safety Manuals and Personal Protective Equipment (PPE), if necessary.
- Library Facility Security Procedures: access control; key cards and ID badges; opening/closing times; burglar, fire, and panic alarms (if in use).
- Emergency procedures: fires, weather emergencies, natural disasters, 9-1-1 calls, workplace violence evacuations.
- Employee Assistance Program (EAP) provider, if applicable; employee wellness programs and services.

I'm assuming here that these are people hired into the library from the outside, not from within the library branch system. Obviously, the orientation process for an employee moving across town to start at another branch is an easier approach. And as a related point, your onboarding efforts are different if you are only bringing one new employee into the library, as opposed to six at a time. Adjust your approach by the size of the group.

For a small to midsize group, consider the value of bringing the new employees into the library for a half-day (paid) orientation. You can give them all of their HR-related forms and documents, copies of benefits packages, and the Employee Manual and/or Policies and Procedures Manual at that time, and explain that they don't need to read and sign everything on this first half-day. Spend the rest of this short work period just taking them around the facility, introducing them (give them a name tag as soon as you shake their hand in welcome), and letting them watch how the library operates, both on the floor and in the back offices. A half-day seems to be a useful span, with just enough information and a reasonable number of things to see and hear, versus too much data and visuals, crammed into one long and confusing day.

Day Two of orientation/onboarding can follow a full-day work schedule, with individual and small-group meetings and any required trainings. I've always found it useful, motivational, and even a bit inspirational, to have the new employees greeted as a group by the library director and every leader on down (plus you, in your HR role), including the PICs. No need for long speeches during these introductions. It's more about every leader offering some abbreviated version of: Who I am, what I do, who works for me, and welcome to the library. This also gives the leaders a chance to speak about what's important to them, hopefully brag a bit about the skills and successes of their departments or teams, and talk about how the various groups fit together and serve each other, directly and indirectly.

We want the new hires to put names to faces, including introducing themselves to their new colleagues, and sharing some information that helps lessen the stress by looking for common ground during those early moments.

It's no surprise that many new employees feel uncomfortable asking questions about matters related to their medical benefits, tax forms, pay periods, direct deposits, and other financials. Set aside one-on-one meeting time with each person, in those first few days, so they don't have to share their personal concerns with the group. Promise them all that although you'll provide a lot of information in a short period of time, you will always make time for their questions and answers, especially during those private meetings.

ORIENTING AND ONBOARDING THE STAFF AND FIRST-LINE SUPERVISOR LEVELS

When I describe "Biggest Orientation Need," it's under the assumption that the new hires' basic HR needs have been already met—from the bullet points above and including your own site-specific additions. I'm not being cryptic here, just emphasizing the core issue(s) that new people, in new jobs, need most.

Volunteer/Part-Time Employee. Biggest Orientation Need: Their specific job duties, work roles, and shift responsibilities; flexible work schedules; and who do I report to?

Full-Time Staff—Patron Contact Position. Biggest Orientation Need: Their specific job duties, work roles, and shift responsibilities; fixed or flexible work schedules; how to support their patron-contact co-workers; and who do I report to?

Full-Time Staff—Non-Patron Contact, Limited Contact, or Back Office Position. Biggest Orientation Need: Their specific job duties, work roles, and shift responsibilities; work schedules; how to support their back office co-workers; and who do I report to?

New PIC. Biggest Orientation Need: Operational Guidelines; opening and closing the facility; enforcing the Code of Conduct; patron use policies; the specific job duties, work roles, and patron services; and facility responsibilities of the staff on shift.

Supervisor. Biggest Orientation Need: The roles and responsibilities of their PICs and the staff.

ORIENTING AND ONBOARDING THE LEADERSHIP LEVELS: SOME FINE POINTS

There can be a tendency, once people reach these levels in an organization, to overload them with information or ask for decisions, before they've had a chance to look around, settle in, and see who is who, and what is what. No one wants or likes to drink from a firehose Day One or Week One. Unless there is a critical need or an urgency to their work, let them digest and observe things, sit in on meetings—without having to do much more than just introduce themselves and listen to the proceedings. There will be time soon enough for them to demonstrate their influence and leadership skills. Don't let them get into a position where they harm their early reputation by trying to do too much and end up rubbing people the wrong way or disturbing what is a reasonably stable work culture.

Four themes for them to follow here, at every leadership level:

First, Seek to Understand.
Second, Don't Fix What Isn't Broken.
Third, Make Small Changes Over Time.
Fourth, They Already Know You're in Charge; Exert Your Influence Carefully.

Manager. Biggest Orientation Need: Roles and Responsibilities of Their Subordinates.

Department Head. Biggest Orientation Need: The roles and responsibilities of their managers and supervisors; and their goals, based on the Library's Strategic Plan.

Deputy/Assistant/Associate Director. Biggest Orientation Need: Data.

Since much of the work at this level is at the behest, direction, and discretion of their boss, the orientation process should focus on their job duties and responsibilities, the director's presumed expectations, and the elements of the library's strategic plan. Leaders at this level need to know the truth, so they can help their director make competent decisions. It's not useful to overload them with a mountain of data that can't be digested easily or quickly. They will want to know about budget issues; the financial health of the library; any immediate HR and staffing concerns; the issues that concern the various communities who use the library; and who is who, both on the organizational chart, and in the political world on the perimeter of their library. These people are often asked to represent the director and reinforce her or his messages and directions to these various stakeholders.

Library Director. Biggest Orientation Need: Early Support.

Assign a competent administrative assistant to the new Big Boss during her or his orientation week. This person must be able to read situations and gently and politely step in to redirect certain energies or decisions if the director is about to veer off course because of constant distractions and people overload. I have met plenty of extroverted library directors in my travels and they are pure extroverts. I have met some library directors who were absolute introverts and seemed both inwardly and outwardly miserable when their quotient of human contact and stressful situations was reached, long before day's end. The largest segment of library leaders I've seen are more like me—an introvert trapped in an extrovert's profession. We like people and being social, just not all the time.

A critical part of onboarding a new director is the initial introduction to the staff. Ask any trial attorney about juries getting seated on their first day in the courtroom: people make value judgments based on first impressions.

I saw the new CEO of an engineering firm getting ready to address the entire staff. As the employees were gathering in their seats in a large training room, he began berating the IT techs for their failure to load his PowerPoint slides correctly. Unfortunately, his mic was on and the whole room heard him shouting and cursing. To say the next few moments were awkward when he was finally introduced to the group understates the damage by half. He never recovered from that moment. The employees talked about that scene, and his demeanor on his first day, right up until the moment he was fired, several difficult years later.

The new library director doesn't need a babysitter, but she or he could benefit from a well-placed, confident but tactful assistant to help her or him get through the first week or so, by running interference, reminding the director of people's names and roles, and just making sure things run smoothly until she or he can take full control.

USING YOUR BEST EMPLOYEES AS SHADOW
MENTORS, TRAINERS, AND GUIDES

"This will get better. With a bit more keyboard time and practice, you'll get the hang of our software. Not every patron is this much of an obnoxious jerk as the guy you just had to deal with." Imagine you're a new library employee, who has never worked in the library field or at a branch, and that is what a caring and concerned co-worker tells you after a particularly rough day, filled with errors and missteps.

Fit matters, when it comes to who you assign to mentor, train, guide, or orient your new hires. Maybe you have someone on your HR team who is empathic, enthusiastic, and patient, making them the perfect person for this role. Maybe it's a longtime PIC, who has seen and done it all, but hasn't become burned out and impatient with patrons and colleagues. Maybe, instead of being a manager, supervisor, or PIC, it's a longtime employee, who is beloved by all and relishes the role of bringing new people into the library world. Pick wisely; they will have a huge impact on this new person.

In my perfect HR world, this onboarding trainer would be both a voluntary and a selected position, with a pay boost to match the amount and importance of the work. It's the rare employee who doesn't mind having extra duties added to her or his day, and if this person complains, it's mostly inwardly. More likely, it's the ones who howl aloud about having to "drag someone new around the library all day, teach them how to do everything, and not get a dime's extra out of the effort," whom we want to avoid.

Selecting this person to escort, shadow, inform, support, and praise new employees should start as a memo or email to HR as to why they are interested in fulfilling this role. You'll need to review their previous Performance Evaluations to see if they are working at a level we want. (Poor performers have a nasty habit of leaking out their frustration about the organization and/ or certain people in it, which is not what we want a new hire to hear. No need to create doubts in the person's mind or worse, have them agree with the brainwashing and start to resent the library and her or his co-workers without cause or even enough time to judge it all.)

To prevent grumblings about being given more to do, add a title and an hourly or salary pay bump to make this role more enticing. "Onboarding Trainer," "Support Team Trainer," or "Orientation Team Trainer" all have a nice ring to them. We need to spell out the job duties for this role; it's not to be a glorified babysitter or a paid listener while the new hire vents about how tough it all is.

Once we have a list, we can use an informal group interview with the interested candidates all together, to talk about the goals, and the tasks and duties our newest employees should know and be able to accomplish.

After the group discussion, we can select a smaller collection of the most qualified people for the job and set one-on-one interviews to help finalize our choices. We're looking for employee-trainers who have enough years of experience; knowledge of the facility, library work, and service to patrons; good speaking skills; and an enthusiasm to train people and demonstrate why it's a good place to work.

The opposite alternative—an employee who didn't volunteer for the new hire orientation role, and it shows in her or his tone, body language, and visible lack of enthusiasm—is the absolute wrong choice. We don't need someone who will lie and tell a new hire that library work is always joyful and fun, but we don't want someone leading the new hire around and causing that person to wonder if she or he made a terrible mistake by coming aboard.

It can help if we first develop a "Critical Task List" for the trainer to help the trainee complete, within a reasonable period. Finishing this checklist of "The Basics" means the employee doing the training feels comfortable that the new hire has enough early knowledge to be able to work without constant supervision.

Choose your training ambassadors, those supporters of a nourishing workplace culture, our most positive role models, carefully. Thank them for their knowledge, enthusiasm, and for representing your facility with grace to the people who want and need to see a friendly face at that critical part of their careers.

THE VALUE OF CONNECTION, CAMARADERIE, AND COHESION

We can get employees to do hard, messy, nasty, loud, uncomfortable, and even dangerous things—cleaning septic tanks, loading airline bags in a snowstorm (ask me), washing dishes (ditto), making sheet metal, dealing with crabby, entitled library patrons, or fighting forest fires—if they have been properly and fully trained to do it; have the equipment and tools to do it; know why they are doing it; know how it fits into their team, office, department, or company or agency; if they feel supported by their bosses while doing it (which includes seeing their bosses jump in and help do that same difficult work too); if they feel connected to their co-workers; and lastly, if they get real praise after doing the right things, the right way, at the right time.

In the military, the goal of boot camp and basic training is to get the trainees to work in unison. Individuality is not the preferred trait. They are rewarded as a group and punished as a group. They succeed or fail, in many of the exercises, by working together as a group or not doing so. The instructors create themselves as the common enemy, which means they want the recruits to hate being yelled at, so much so that they band together and get the work, drills, or tactical problems done as a team.

While this is not the best approach in a library ("Drop and give me twenty push-ups before you shelve those books!"), it points to the value of team-work, and especially a harmonious team. The creation of cohesive groups starts at the top and it starts early.

By far, the two biggest and most detailed complaints I ever hear from employees about new hires are: (1) "This person was either not prepared to do this job, didn't want to learn how to do it, or was not taught how to do it. As such, they are miserable and they make other people miserable." (2) "This person should have never been allowed to pass probation. It's clear they don't want to be here. Maybe they're just sticking around because of the pay, or more likely, to get the medical benefits. But now that they've made it beyond probation, they feel like they can say or do whatever they want. Most of us wish they would go work somewhere else. The fact that senior management or HR has allowed them to continue is a disturbing concern for all of us."

Shame on us, as HR professionals and library leaders, if we don't serve the health of our entire employee culture by screening, selecting, interviewing, and orienting the best people we can find in our communities.

Shame on us if we don't prepare new employees to do the work ahead, so they know what they do matters, to the success of the library, and the success of their colleagues.

As I will discuss in several places in this book, the probationary period is a test for new employees to decide if they can do the work and want to stay. It also gives us a way to measure those same things and to support them if we agree they can contribute and excuse them from future work here if they can't or won't. Our effort should be to create a thorough, detailed, structured, and even a bit demanding onboarding and orientation process (e.g., failing to complete the Critical Task List after several attempts is grounds for dismissal). It should serve the new employees and the existing ones. Anything less is a disservice to both.

THE COMING OF A BRIGHTER DAY

At the end of the orientation process, we'd like new employees to say some version of the following, to themselves: "This appears to be a safe, stable, professional place to work. I made the right choice by coming to work here. These leaders are here to help me fit in right away, so I can do my job and help the patrons and my co-workers."

This should be a time to welcome them and set expectations; to provide them with the same rules of accountability, responsibility, and performance as with the current employees; and to speak about our hope for their future success.

It's the best and only opportunity to create a positive and lasting first impression about the library organization. Anything you can do to help them better prepare to work and start off right will be appreciated by the library leaders, department heads, managers, supervisors, and PICs across the organization, along with their colleagues and co-workers.

Chapter 4

Creating Civility in Your Workplace

A New Perspective on Diversity and Conflict Resolution

The concepts that form DEI or DEIB (Diversity-Equity-Inclusion-Belonging) are not easily defined, even by the most well-informed diversity trainer. There are plenty of arguments about the differences between Equity versus Equality and what, exactly, does Belonging mean? The national news media and social media channels have polarized all of these issues into a boiling stewpot of anger, resentment, misunderstandings, and misintentions.

As a library leader at every level, can you teach diversity or should you model it? How about doing both, but in ways that are culturally sensitive and empathic, meaning we don't force employees to change their belief systems under the penalty of career discipline or termination, social ostracization, or opinion cancellation?

I have taught DEI for over twenty-five years and during my training efforts, I have tried to focus on one prevailing theme for all employees who come together and work in an organization: acceptance with understanding, despite differences.

This leads to a question, which is how can someone teach diversity (me included, as an older, edge-of-Baby-Boomer, white male) when they are not a person of color, female, or a member of a historically disenfranchised group? As a psychiatrist might say, "I don't have to be a schizophrenic to treat a schizophrenic."

In other words, an oncologist doesn't have to have cancer to diagnose cancer. I'll agree that I can never see the world from the perspective of someone who has been discriminated against, but I can recognize those behaviors, attitudes, and experiences that have built their own beliefs. And I can train others to be more aware, patient, supportive, and respectful. Within the confines of the training room, I can ask people in protected classes (which go much further than the categories most people think of first: gender, race, or sexual orientation) to volunteer their experiences of being looked down on, talked down to, and held back from the personal and professional success we all deserve.

Let's review the list of potential protected class categories. This list varies from state to state and my former state, California, has the largest collection of categories. This list of eighteen (plus a dozen subcategories) comes from the California State Senate's website (https://www.senate.ca.gov/protected -classes):

- Race
- Color
- Religion (includes religious dress and grooming practices)
- Sex/gender (includes pregnancy, childbirth, breastfeeding, and/or related medical conditions)
- Gender identity, gender expression
- Sexual orientation
- Marital status
- Medical condition (genetic characteristics, cancer, or a record or history of cancer)
- Military or veteran status
- National origin (includes language use and possession of a driver's license issued to persons unable to provide evidence their presence in the United States is authorized under federal law)
- Ancestry
- Disability (mental and physical including HIV/AIDS, cancer, and genetic characteristics)
- Genetic information
- Request for family care leave
- Request for leave for an employee's own serious health condition
- Request for Pregnancy Disability Leave
- Retaliation for reporting patient abuse in tax-supported institutions
- Age (over forty)

Now let's stop to consider two important issues related to being in a protected class:

1. I would argue all adults in US workplaces are in at least one category currently or have been at some point in their careers. Most of us are in several categories, and several of us are in lots and lots of categories. So we need and are legally entitled to support from our bosses and

co-workers, since we are all in one big group of humans with differences and similarities.

2. You can be harassed, discriminated against, or retaliated against in the workplace by bosses, employees, or customers who perceive you're in a protected class, even if you are not. As one example, you have co-workers who are gay and you enjoy going to lunch, getting coffee, and socializing after work with them. Although you aren't gay, any perception that you are by others—that results in harassing, discriminatory, or retaliatory behavior directed at you because of those friendships—is also illegal in our workplaces.

Even people who grew up in the same house have significant differences in how they define themselves when compared to the other people in that home they love and care about. In the workplace, where opposites don't always attract kind feelings between colleagues, my approach has always been to say, "We can coexist, despite any differences we may have or the other person doesn't understand or agree with, because it is the right thing to do for all concerned. We don't have to love or even like each other at work. But we do have to get along, treat each other in professional ways, and serve our library patrons, co-workers, and leaders, and all the other people inside and outside our organization who are counting on us."

What we are asking all employees to do is recognize our differences and appreciate our similarities. First, we want to have acceptance *with* understanding, and then next, understanding *and* acceptance. We realize none of us are perfect in our interpretation of the ever-changing types of cultural, personality, and lifestyle preferences that our employees bring with them into our building each day. Can we all agree to show patience toward our co-workers, who may have questions they want to ask, politely and carefully, to be certain they are not hurting anyone in any way, as they seek to coexist?

CIVILITY AND SOCIAL INTELLIGENCE

I have been testing the concept of civility, which I believe is a useful and powerful element of diversity, with my HR colleagues. Civility, which we can define as the practice of politeness and courtesy in behavior and speech, is perhaps easier to understand and initiate in the workplace because it is rooted in what I would call "professional courtesy, and kindness, no matter the situation," meaning we do it with, for, and around each other because it is the right thing to do. It should be a built-in expectation that we treat all employees this way, up, down, and across the chain of command.

In 2009, my father, Dr. Karl Albrecht, wrote a book for Pfeiffer called *Social Intelligence: The New Science of Success*. In it, he created several models that defined "social intelligence" (SI) in a more thorough way than had been previously, such as in books like Daniel Goleman's 1995 work, *Emotional Intelligence*. While Goleman defined social intelligence as a part of EQ, my dad dug deeper. I think his book offers a unique alternative to Goleman's because it's easier to understand SI. In my training classes where I cover DEIB, conflict resolution, and team success, I define SI in the simplest of terms: "In life and work, personally and professionally, read the room you're in. Say or do the right thing based on who is in the room with you."

This goes beyond just "be nice to other people" or "Do Unto Others," and so on. SI is your ability to not just fit in with the crowd, but to have gathered enough insight so as not to hurt people, harm people, or make your interactions with others worse.

We recognize SI in the people who have it, almost instantly. And we recognize a lack of SI in people who don't have it, just as quickly. What does this mean to us in HR? I use this SI definition as a coaching tool with that group of employees who just don't get it. "No," I tell them, "you can't tell the joke about the camel, the rabbit, and the frog who go into a bar when you're in a room with the mayor of your city, your boss, your boss's boss, and two hundred library patrons. The reason you said that is the reason you're sitting here with me today."

Employees with poor SI often blame others for their own lack of control. "People are too sensitive! I was just kidding around! What's the big deal? Lighten up already!" are their usual defenses. They lack insight and more importantly, they fail to see how their behavior, words, actions, gestures, and physical movements can offend people.

In my perfect library world, HR would model and teach SI, ask the library leaders to do likewise, and demand that all employees follow it. The trailing motto for my definition model of SI should be, "Just because you have the right to do or say something doesn't always mean you should. You don't have the right to press your beliefs, your personality, or your sense of humor onto other people, including our patrons and your co-workers, in our workplace." We have a Code of Civility for our patrons and, just as important, one for our employees too, and it starts with this: "Read the room. Say or do the right thing based on who is in the room with you."

I have managers and supervisors ask me the age-old HR question, "Can we coach, discipline, or terminate an employee for their words, their behaviors, or their actions?" I reply, "Yes! Especially if what they say or do hurts our business, if it interferes with the way we want to run the library."

DR. KARL ALBRECHT'S CODE OF CIVILITY: STEPS FOR HOW WE SHOULD TREAT EACH OTHER

Not surprisingly, based on the bestselling success of his *Social Intelligence* book, my dad created a Code of Civility for the workplace. He published it in a booklet, which he sold to public and private sector firms who gave it to their employees so they could follow the right steps to get along at work.

So much of library work centers around both the outward and the inward customer service experiences: how we treat the patrons and how we treat each other. We exist to serve the public and that part of library service will always be of the most importance.

It also pays dividends to look at how we treat each other, at every level in the library organization. Civility matters, in our interpersonal relationships with each other, whether it's between leaders, with managers and supervisors to their employees, and between employees. From the newest volunteer to the most seasoned library employee, how we treat each other and the type of workplace we create, with conscious efforts, makes a difference in retention, morale, and ultimately, how we take care of our patrons. You want to feel good about coming to work and doing your work (and these are separate and related feelings; you can want to go to work and not want to do your work, both, or neither). Those good feelings can and should rub off on your co-workers.

The work environment we intentionally create becomes something to be proud of. It encourages library applicants to want to apply, new library employees to want to stay, and employees at other branches to want to transfer there. The reverse is true too. When we mistreat each other, when supervisors mistreat employees, or we allow a toxic workplace to grow and saturate the facility, good people quit, other miserable employees stay and make their co-workers miserable, and the reputation around town is, "This Is Not a Good Place to Work." At a time when many public agencies and private sector firms are competing hard to get and keep skilled employees, reputations matter. When we use praise for each other and get it from our bosses, when we treat each other with dignity and respect (not just say it, but demonstrate it, daily), and when we hold ourselves and our leaders accountable to foster and nurture a nourishing workplace, it ends up improving our customer–patron relationships too.

One of the challenges we can encounter when trying to create a civil workplace comes when we create platitudes instead of action statements. The phrase, "We need to respect each other here," sounds great when we say it during a team-building exercise or when we see it on an easel pad page created during a staff meeting (or on one of those motivational posters with trees and lakes and kayaks). The key is to turn an abstract concept—"respect"—into operational behaviors. "Respect each other" means things like returning email messages promptly, making eye contact, not killing new ideas in meetings, and valuing lifestyle differences. It's important to turn ideas into tools everyone can use.

The following "Code of Civility," created by my father, Dr. Karl Albrecht (www.KarlAlbrecht.com), offers a set of ten practical steps we can put to use today, to help us to get along. These are not just "words about polite workplace behaviors"; we need to use our forum in HR to help our leaders model these ideas, and help them help the staff turn these civility themes into observable actions. Consider these ten civility behaviors for your library:

In our library organization . . .

1. Our library leaders model and encourage a culture of civility.
2. We treat each other with respect, courtesy, and consideration.
3. We value the small courtesies of everyday life.
4. We value the diversity in people, ideas, and points of view.
5. We can disagree agreeably—we don't personalize or emotionalize our differences.
6. We resolve misunderstandings maturely, without accusing, blaming, or finger-pointing.
7. We cooperate between work groups, not putting fences between us.
8. We play fair, not letting destructive office politics divide us.
9. We share information and knowledge, understanding that they are valuable assets.
10. We expect each other to act as good citizens of our library organization.

It's never enough just to post these on your Intranet, or in a poster in the employee break room (along with the 382 HR compliance-related posters already there), and hope the employees at all levels somehow get the concepts. These are abstract themes (respect, courtesy, cooperation, being a good citizen of our library) and as such they need to be introduced, discussed, and even demonstrated in the training environment. Wearing your HR training hat, you can and should facilitate how these ten approaches are to be demonstrated, staff-wide and by every leader. This can include whole-group discussions of the Civility Code definitions, small-group work to isolate individual examples to be shared with the room, and easel pad work to make the ideas real. While my dad would be thrilled if you bought individual copies of the booklets he created that explain each of the ten concepts in detail, he would want you to operationalize them even more.

GENERATIONAL CLASHES: AGE AS A COVERT OR OVERT CONFLICT CREATOR

Consider your current circle of friends, not just family, relatives, work colleagues, or casual acquaintances, but people you define as either a best friend or close friends. For me, that number is six, all men I have known for spans of time ranging from fifty-five to twenty-five years. With each, we have both made a long-ago spoken (and proven, many times) agreement that I would do anything necessary for that person if he asks and he will do anything I ask for me. Some of the six know each other well, others not at all. They are nearly as dear to me as my own family. If you have one or more people like those in your life you can trust to be your friend 'til death, you are blessed.

Now consider that you may have various similarities in character, values, political beliefs, socioeconomic standing, life skills, educational and professional backgrounds, and cultural or geographic upbringings, as well as completely opposite characteristics in those areas. No matter, you love them for who they are and vice versa. But the one area you are probably most similar in life with your closest friends is in your ages. We mostly associate the closest with people plus or minus five years from our own age. You can certainly have younger friends and older friends, but not that much on either side of your age. People who are fifty-two don't usually hang around people who are twenty-two. There are exceptions, but it's not the rule. We most often connect initially and stay around people who have shared some portion of the same iconic, generational, and cultural moments (especially involving music, movies, books, tragic and uplifting national events, concerts, and TV shows). Birds of a feather flock together. (The music you liked in high school you probably still like today. I grew up in the Disco Era, so there goes that theory.)

Baby Boomers (1946–1964)
Generation X (1965–1980)
Generation Y Millennials (1981–1996)
Generation Z (1997–2011)
Generation Alpha (2012–2025)

In organizations where I consult, I have witnessed generational differences as a significant and seemingly hidden source of conflict between employees. More than a few leaders, managers, and supervisors failed to recognize that collisions of perception based on age were the real cause of the team and individual conflicts. Don't discount the impact of large age gaps between employees as one primary reason they may not get along, respect each other, or even trust each other.

From the HR office, we must pay careful attention to the warning signs of these dividers: giving each other the silent treatment; being dismissive of their opinions, especially in meetings; idea-killing their fledgling ideas in staff meetings or training sessions; using sarcastic or mean-spirited jokes, said to or near the group members, or spread on the Intranet as cartoons, videos, or memes; and most commonly, when you hear or see so many examples of frustrated employees complaining to you or others' bosses that "this person" or "those people" don't get them, the goals, or the work culture. And remember the root cause of these collisions is because of the age strata differences, not usually any other protected class category.

We may see six possible types of employee-to-employee or boss-to-employee conflicts in our modern workplaces:

- Younger employees frustrated with older employees: "Why won't they use more technology? Why does everything take so long with them? Look it up on your phone!"
- Older employees frustrated with younger employees: "Where is their work ethic? Not everything can be found on Google!"
- Older employees frustrated with younger bosses: "They don't appreciate the time we have spent here, building this place and this work culture. They complain our solutions are outdated, even when they still work just fine."
- Older bosses frustrated with younger employees: "Why don't they get here on time? Why can't they meet our deadlines, with the quality we expect?"
- Younger employees frustrated with older bosses: "We don't need to have yet another staff meeting! Why can't I work from home, at least a few days per week?"
- Younger bosses frustrated with older employees: "Why are so many of my older employees dismissive, intolerant, or avoidant of better, faster technology? Why do they insist on doing things harder, slower, and less efficiently?"

There are countless variations of these generational gap questions or complaints, which really ask the universal question, "Why can't this person be more like me?"

So the question you might ask yourself and the supervisors of employees who are in conflict or even at war with each other is, "Could the source of their disagreements be based on age differences? Not race, gender, religion, sexual orientation, or any other protected class? Could it simply be that each employee sees the ocean through his or her own generational drinking straw?"

This means there is a lack of understanding that interferes with their work relationship. Those reasons are primary, meaning they are hard to fix with just by having HR say, "Hey! You all need to get along!"

It will take coaching conversations, small-group meetings, and the courage to be honest about the frustrations each has with the others, not so they can get worse, but so there can be the start of some understanding.

A MODEL FOR TWO-EMPLOYEE CONFLICT RESOLUTION

As an issue that often requires HR interventions, conflicts between two employees is about as event-driven as it gets. I've yet to see an HR director or a library director bring me in when everyone is getting along fine. I have worked with successful, high-performing, or cohesive teams and there are many reasons they don't need conflict resolution help: they communicate directly with each other, using honest, timely feedback; they talk before small problems grow too large; they set mutual personal boundaries with each other, about how they expect to be treated, respected, and communicated with; and they didn't always need help from HR or their bosses to get back to work.

When your employees will not or cannot get along, and refuse every effort to solve it themselves, you will either need to intervene and facilitate a series of problem-solving discussions or train your managers and supervisors to do it. You can already guess the latter is not a task most bosses want to tackle, because of their sense of emotionality, anger, frustration, no apparent solutions, and no end in sight. "Have HR fix them" is the common refrain. If so, let's tackle how you get two employees to at least tolerate each other for the time they are in the same room or the same building.

Some employees just get on each other's nerves. As much as we say, urge, and ask all employees to get along in the time and space they are together, there are a few who can't or won't and this will probably require you to intervene (see "their reluctant bosses" above). Our usual speech is this: "Look, you don't have to love each other, like each other, or socialize together. You do have to coexist and cooperate. I expect it from HR, your boss expects it, your co-workers would appreciate it, and our patrons and the community we serve expect it too." At this stage, when each employee can't even stand to be in the same room as the other, the time for you or their bosses to "coach them up" has passed and we need to move into conflict resolution mode.

The key to success in these meetings is not to focus on who is wrong or right, going back ten years to bring up old sagas, or who has the right to keep score or hold a never-ending grudge. The focus should be on moving forward by agreeing on a set of ground rules. These are guidelines that both employees can agree to follow (no matter how grudgingly) from now on, that don't require you or their bosses to constantly monitor their interactions. We're asking them to behave like adults working in a professional environment. (How hard can that be? Turns out, it's pretty hard.)

The suggested process below requires patience, empathy, good communication and facilitation skills on your part, patience, and in case we forgot to mention it twice, more patience. It starts with several one-on-one discussions that you need to have with each employee, and it ends with a meeting between all three of you. The outcome (not a "poutcome," as one of our colleagues suggested, when both employees leave the room and go pout) should be to agree to abide by the ground rules you have all agreed upon.

Employees at war with each other don't usually want to participate in any discussion when the other person is in the room. On occasion, one will want to meet with you and sort things out and the other won't, which gives the first employee the chance to tell you how he or she is morally superior and/or rub it in the other employee's face, "See! I wanted to meet but he or she didn't! Who has the problem now? Not me!" Mostly, though, both employees should agree to meet with you alone, as many times as necessary to get all of the issues out, then meet together to solidify the agreed ground rules.

Some employees in the union or association will believe this is a discipline meeting and will want a rep present. It's not a "leading to discipline—Weingarten meeting," where the employee needs a union or association rep. These are coaching meetings where the focus is on resolving conflicts between two employees. They are not discipline meetings and should be treated and discussed as such, with both, in advance of the first and each subsequent meeting. Do not reference the possibility of discipline in any of these meetings and never threaten them by saying, "You two had better get along, or else one or both of you is going to be looking at some days off!"

It's tough enough to facilitate a meeting with two employees who already don't get along. Can you imagine the tension if they each bring a rep into the room? Don't position these meetings as anything other than a series of coaching meetings with a conflict resolution goal. Any discipline options should only occur long after it's clear that the ground rules didn't work as planned and their relationship has continued to escalate into PIPs, BIPs, or written warnings.

My approach to employee conflict resolution works well when it's done with skill (and it takes practice to do it well). It demands that you follow a structured approach. It's not just a chat; there are rules for them to follow and work they must do. The changes are driven by the employees, not just by you telling or ordering them to get along. When they can agree upon the ground rules and then their need to follow them, the buy-in is theirs, not just yours. Your function, besides carefully facilitating the meetings, is to listen to the suggested ground rules (or make your own if they are hesitant or get stuck) and fine-tune their ideas into a workable compromise.

Here are some examples of ground rules, as they need to be created, spoken, and used by the two employees. It's not about you telling them what to do to get along as much as it is for them to develop them to live and work by. Ground rules can range from professional work requests to behavioral boundaries to ways to smooth personality differences. There are lots of examples, which the two employees should articulate to you in the first separate meetings you have, and then talk with each other about them in the final, facilitated group meeting:

"We agree to return each other's phone calls, emails, or work texts within twenty-four hours."

"You agree not to touch me in any way."

"I'll agree not to make or have loud speakerphone calls near your desk."

"I agree to clean up the Reference Desk work area before I turn it over to you."

"We agree to not give each other the silent treatment and communicate about work issues when it's needed."

Consider this structured approach to conflict resolution between Employee #1 and Employee #2. The order is important, so try not to deviate from it.

1. Meet with Employee #1 alone. Ask what Employee #2 does to make it hard to get along or get her/his work done. Get specific answers, using examples, not just labels or sweeping generalizations ("He always . . ." or "She never . . .") Help Employee #1 to start to craft some potential ground rules for you to be able to share with Employee #2 in a future meeting.
2. Meet with Employee #2 alone. Ask what Employee #1 does to make it hard to get along or get her/his work done. Get specific examples. Help Employee #2 to craft some potential ground rules for you to be able to share with Employee #1 in a future meeting.
3. Meet with Employee #1 and #2 separately again and discuss the ground rules each has suggested for the other. Fine-tune these requests until there is a full understanding of the language and what is being asked of the other employee. These individual ground rules meetings are the key to the success of this approach. Write the ground rules down for each person, if you think that will cement them. Use your HR expertise to help craft realistic, fair, and legal ground rules.
4. At the end of this meeting with each person, discuss whether Employee #1 and Employee #2 need a final meeting, facilitated by you, to explain fully the ground rules. If they don't want to meet, tell them you expect complete compliance with the ground rules, starting immediately, and that you will hold both of them accountable for what they agreed upon in your presence.

5. If both employees agree to a mutual meeting to finalize the ground rules, set that meeting and explain your role: "This meeting is between the two of you. I'll be there to facilitate the discussion and not let things get out of control or deteriorate. We will be civil and polite in this meeting. No shouting, no storming out of the room, no tears, and most importantly, you will face each other—and not look just at me—and discuss your ground rules."

This last instruction is a critical one because too many times, the employees will sit across the table from each other and then proceed to review the ground rules with you, not each other. It's important that they each own the meeting and the future requested results with each other. If they try to turn and face you when they should be looking at the other person, get them back on track.

Some frontline supervisors will resist conducting the process we have just described because it can be anything from easy to excruciating to meet with both employees in the same room for the final "Come Together" discussion where they (hopefully) agree to coexist. It's not a requirement that you all meet as a group of three and discuss the ground rules, but it works much better that way.

Make it crystal clear to each employee that they are not being "forced by HR or my boss to sit in a room with a co-worker I can't stand." You aren't coercing them, under the threat of discipline. They can choose not to participate in the final meeting and they can leave that final meeting if the tension gets too high. It's not a hostage situation; it's a ground rules discussion and they should be willing to do the work necessary to make things at least a bit better than they have been for the past weeks, months, or even years.

Do what you need to do to control this final meeting and protect both employees from verbally attacking each other. Keep the focus on the acceptance of the ground rules. You or their boss may need to meet with them separately and/or together at some point in the future to remind them of the agreed-upon ground rules or to fine-tune them for even more lasting compliance and cooperation.

Chapter 5

Supporting Your Managers and Supervisors with Coaching Skills Training

Developing Your Coaching Toolkit

When it comes to coaching employees to improve either their work performance or their work behavior, as an HR professional, you will have one of three paths: coach the employee, on behalf of your leaders, managers, and supervisors; train your leaders, managers, and supervisors to coach their own employees, to reach mutually agreed-upon performance and/or behavior standards; or do a little bit of both. (The fourth alternative—hope the employees themselves figure out how to be or get better at their jobs on their own and without feedback, guidance, and support—is not a viable route.)

There are benefits and drawbacks to these two approaches:

Pro: Coaching library employees from within your HR office gives you a wide sense of what is happening in the building and an easier read on both the health of the work culture and the emotional temperature when it comes to employee interactions with each other and with patrons.

Con: Coaching all the employees in your library who need it can be time-intensive, exhausting, and hard to remember who said what to whom, when, and why.

Pro: Training your leaders, managers, and supervisors can free up your time, drive them toward more accountability and responsibility for the success of their people, and give you both the business results you're all looking for.

Con: Two issues: First, some leaders, managers, and supervisors don't enjoy the coaching process and despite your efforts to train them, give them plenty of role-play work and role-play scenarios in a protected environment with you, they just don't, or won't get the value of coaching. Some don't like having to have difficult, stressful, or consequence-based conversations with their people, preferring to "have HR do it, since it's probably going to turn into discipline anyway." As a result, they try to defer complicated employee issues (which may have been brewing for months or even years) back on to you.

And in a related issue, we have to ask ourselves, "Where do the majority of managers and supervisors even get coaching training and enough experience to do it well?" The answer is "on the job." Rare is the boss who has been through a formalized training program. (I earned my coaching certification through an intensive cohort program run by Fielding Graduate University. Lots of study, writing, and role-play practice with my colleagues for that one.) Most frontline supervisors get their coaching experience starting with "corrective discussions," designed to get the employee to stop doing something and start doing something else. Those are hard conversations, especially when compared to the easier, more positive, and even fun ones, related to mentoring, career development, helping employees who want to promote to the next level, and the highest form of coaching, succession planning. It may be up to you to provide the training and experience-gathering they need.

Second, there are some library leaders, managers, and supervisors who believe coaching is just not possible anymore because of either union MOUs or their (mis)understanding of the library's HR policy on progressive discipline. They wrongly believe they can't have a conversation of a counseling or corrective nature with an employee because it somehow violates union agreements or HR policies, "because once you start asking them or telling them to work differently, it becomes a discipline conversation."

This is simply not true. Even the strictest interpretation of Memos of Understanding (MOUs) still allows bosses to meet with their employees and talk about gaps in their performance or behavior. The key is not to threaten discipline during the coaching meeting, as in, "You better change or you're gonna get fired!" That's not how HR operates. What you need to tell and remind your cadre of library bosses, at every level, is that they have every right to ask for performance improvement or behavioral changes with their employees, using as many coaching conversations as it takes to see those changes. We should give our employees encouragement, examples, training, and time to improve. Once that has not worked, then and only then do we switch to progressive discipline (as I will discuss in chapter 6).

Good bosses, at every level, coach their employees, formally and informally, every day. It's as simple as that. You already know that bosses who make excuses, invent rationalizations, or dismiss coaching efforts behind bogus fears about legal, union, or HR restrictions are those who are failing to lead. Not taking the daily opportunity to fine-tune how people work, behave, serve, interact, and perform is leadership malpractice.

Let's be honest, shall we? When it comes to the need for coaching, most library managers and supervisors know already who are the star performers, the poor performers, and those in between, just by direct observations. If they have watched the work activities, service to the patrons, and interactions with and support of their co-workers for at least ninety days, they have reached certain conclusions about who works extra hard, who works at a satisfactory level, who works at a basic level, and who just shows up and does no apparent work at all. They can measure positive attitudes, built-in motivations, and the lack thereof, just by watching and listening to what goes on around them.

When I worked as a supervisor for the city of San Diego, we had a program in one of the departments that measured at-risk employees, based on about fifteen performance or behavior issues. This data was gathered regularly and compiled in a database only the managers and supervisors could access. Employees in the "Blue Zone" or the "top 5%" were the ones thought to be the most in need of coaching. I did the training for the senior leaders about the measurements and when I asked them if they could predict who would be in the blue area, they were not-so-astonishingly correct in their guesses, every time. They already knew, at a highly intuitive level, who needed coaching, who needed discipline, who was on a rising trajectory for their career path, and who needed to be let go.

What your managers and supervisors do with that eyewitness information is the critical part. Do they act on it, getting the full support of HR? Do they wait for HR or other senior leaders to call out what needs to be done? Do they ignore it and hope the employees who present the most performance and behavior issues will somehow self-correct? We know what most often happens when bad things are left unchecked. It takes management courage to initiate the changes the coaching seeks to support.

DEFINING COACHING

We can define coaching as, "One or more pre-discipline conversations about performance or behavior." Notice the prominent phrase "pre-discipline." This is where many inexperienced managers and supervisors fail to grasp the coaching concept because they continue to see coaching as a black/white, yes/no, do/do not process, where they have to gain the employee's compliance on the first conversation or otherwise it's a failure.

Or that the employee's lack of compliance—which is often due to a training gap or a lack of understanding—means that discipline is the next step. If you're an experienced, patient, empathic leader, you have certainly coached some of your people for years before they "got it." A CEO once told me, "I came home from work and told my dog to stop sleeping on my couch every day for a year. On the 366th day, I came home and he wasn't sleeping on the couch. Things take time with some people." (And some dogs.)

To be successful in the coaching process, we need to answer the "WII-FM?" question for each of our employees, as in, "What's in it for me?" We are all selfishly concerned with our own success, so it helps to explain the why of coaching to employees, both with them alone, and as part of staff meetings, where they can all hear the same messages.

We coach our employees because:

- It lets them know where they stand when it comes to many facets of their jobs.
- It helps them "rescue their careers" if they are moving toward discipline or termination.
- It tells them what, specifically, they need to improve. (And even our shining stars/rising stars have room for growth and development.)
- It helps them set their own personal, professional, and educational goals.
- It helps management and HR identify skill gaps, training needs, and ways to improve their overall job knowledge.
- It shows them what they need to do to promote, or move into other leadership positions or specific assignments, if they so desire.
- It helps senior management to explain the strategic goals they're trying to set, the longer-term direction for the library, and how all that fits into the city/county or library district's strategic plan.
- It gives managers and supervisors an entry point to solve conflicts between two or more employees or between work teams.
- It helps bosses and/or HR meet proactively with at-risk employees, especially those having significant personal problems where they can make appropriate or urgent referrals to the library's Employee Assistance Program (EAP) provider.
- It helps library leaders and HR meet proactively with employees who are on the fast track to promotions.
- It makes it easier for all bosses to do an accurate and fair performance evaluation on their behalf.
- It rewards them by recognizing them for their efforts and accomplishments.
- It helps library leaders and HR to initiate mentorship programs that can help with succession planning (as senior leaders move up, out, or start to retire).

PROVING COACHING WORKS

How do we demonstrate success in our coaching efforts? There are lots of markers: we see policy and behavioral compliance; we see improvement in the employee's work quality; we see positive changes in his or her attitude, interactions, initiative, responsibility, and accountability. In other words, they start doing the jobs we originally hired them to do, with safety, skill, and self-direction.

For our work teams and library departments, we can use coaching for: group behavior and/or performance improvement; creating negotiated "get along" agreements between teams or departments that aren't cooperating; conflict resolution between two employees who need to get along but won't; and for overall team success, by using coaching to provide praise and build employee morale for continuous good work.

We can use coaching to identify a hidden skill gap or a missed training gap. How many training gaps might exist with your people, that are known by everyone but you and not said or unknown by everyone, including you, because the employee is good at hiding her or his deficiencies?

OBSTACLES TO COACHING

So if all of this is so important to the growth and development of your employees, and the continued success of our library leaders, managers, and supervisors, do we need to talk about it so much? Doesn't every boss at every level in the organization use her or his coaching skills with her or his team or department? The short answer is no and it can be complex as to why not.

There is something we can call "The Supervisor's Paradox," which has three parts. The first issue is that some supervisors don't use coaching early enough and when they finally do, it's often too late to do anything other than move into discipline. Things went along until things failed and then it became time for discipline. Hard feelings emerged on all sides because most HR people knew this all could have been prevented through early coaching interventions.

The second issue stopping supervisors and leaders from coaching is a hard one—especially for new bosses—to swallow. Tell your leaders, managers, and supervisors to print this out and tape it over your desk:

YOU WILL HAVE TO SPEND MORE TIME COACHING EMPLOYEES WHO ALREADY DRIVE YOU CRAZY.

They must face two facts early: (1) Your rising stars/shining stars don't need much coaching. They already do their jobs to your satisfaction; that's why we enjoy being around them (and putting them in charge when we aren't around). (2) The employees who get on our last nerve are the ones who need the most help.

Your bosses will have to spend time coaching the people they don't really want to spend time coaching. But that's what leaders do; they prepare for and move into difficult, crucial conversations, because they realize these employees won't self-correct and what they do or don't do hurts the business of their library. They must steel themselves for the necessary coaching meetings with their most challenging, problematic, irascible, sarcastic, complaining, under-motivated, or difficult employees; those who most need their help, whether they will admit it or not. They will need to meet with them proactively, whether they like them or not. Liking them or not is not the issue; seeking competence through supportive coaching is.

And keep in mind there is a ***self-fulfilling prediction*** in all this. HR needs to help its leaders ask and answer this question: "Does what you ***think*** about your employees, positively or negatively, have any effect on their motivation or performance?" Expectations are a powerful thing. How we expect people to work is generally how they actually work. If we think they will fail, they just might. If we think they will succeed, then they probably will. We often coach, supervise, manage, and lead with a set of pre-determined expectations already in mind and those often happen.

The third reason some leaders, managers, or supervisors don't want to coach or don't like to coach is something called the "Inverse Reward System."

This rears its ugly head, especially when a frontline supervisor asks for help with a particularly challenging employee and is told to "handle it yourself" by the senior leaders. As the most common example, a newer or younger library supervisor asks her or his boss for help with an employee whom she or he is having work performance or behavior problems with. Instead of hearing, "Come on in. Close the door. Let's talk about what we can do together to bring your subordinate back up to full speed," the response is, "Why can't you supervise that person as well as you supervise the others?"

This shoot-the-messenger approach can encourage many supervisors not to bring performance or behavior concerns to their bosses for help, until, and you can guess the rest, the issues get severe and the next phase of the Inverse Reward System kicks in. First, we have top management apathy or resistance toward supporting their own supervisors, until something happens, and then the message is, "Why didn't you come to me/us sooner? Look at the size of this mess now!"

Being in a leadership position in HR, you need to make certain you do not use the Inverse Reward System on your leaders at every level and that they don't use it on the supervisors who work for them.

DEFINING THE IMPACT ON OUR BUSINESS

It can be useful to look at the need for coaching as it connects to the concept of "business impact." We can use this measure to ask our library leaders,

"How do we operate in ways that impact the business of our library in positive ways? How do we avoid patron service issues or employee problems that impact our business in negative ways?"

When it comes to the need for coaching, we can ask similar questions, specific to the behavior or performance of certain employees: Is what they are doing or not doing hurting our business or helping it? An employee who is constantly rude and generates a lot of patron (and co-worker) complaints hurts our business. A PIC who is not managing her or his shift of employees hurts our business. An employee who has discussed having a trauma background and is now letting it hurt her or his service relationship with patrons or colleagues may need help about getting help. Those business impact issues require us to step in as leaders and coaches.

COACHING OPPORTUNITIES

We can adapt our communication approaches with our employees by varying our coaching methods. Some coaching takes place on the spot—what we call "corridor coaching"—as in catching the employee in the hallway and saying, "Can we talk about something you said during the staff meeting?" We can coach our employees on a much more informal basis, sitting over a cup of tea in the break room, with the door closed. If the situation is serious enough, we may need to coach employees in our offices, with the door closed and with the person sitting in front of our Big Important Desks, while we sit in Our Big Important Chairs. Those types of meetings are serious and could be the type that leads to discipline later.

Management guru Tom Peters is famous for a book he wrote in 1982 with Bob Waterman called *In Search of Excellence*.[1] He coined the term MBWA or Management By Walking Around. (Other wags have called it Management By Wandering Around, which fits too.) We can coach employees in low-key, informal situations, based on what we see and hear in the stacks, during staff meetings, during training classes, and at other times where we view (or stagger into) issues that call for it.

We can coach by phone, which lacks the important body language and eye contact elements but may be the most timely or convenient. We can certainly coach via Zoom or Teams, especially since we can see and hear the person. (The employees will have to agree to show us their faces during these online meetings; otherwise, just use the phone.) We can and should coach by email, because it gives our employees time to consider our words, and respond accordingly, and it provides them and us with the added bonus of protecting, documenting, and memorializing our words for future reference by both sides.

We can even coach by text. It may not be the preferred approach of older bosses, but consider that for many Gen Y or Gen Z employees, it may be the communication method they like the most. Why? It's less intrusive for them, provides less of a face-to-face intensity, and besides, they're already carrying their smartphones around all day anyway.

TWO COACHING COMMUNICATION TOOLS

We will talk about how to structure coaching meetings a bit later on in this chapter. For now, consider two tools that can help you focus on organizing the content of your employee meetings. The first is called "The Keep / Stop / Start Tool" and it can simplify your thoughts as to how to talk to even the most difficult employees. You can either ask these three as questions or turn them into statements:

> "What should you KEEP doing, because it's working?" or "Here's what I'd / we'd like you to keep doing, because it's good for you and what we're trying to do here."

> "What should you STOP doing, because it's not working?" or "Here's what I'd / we'd like you to stop doing, because it's not good for you and not useful for what we are trying to do here."

> "What should you START doing, because it will work better?" or "Here's what I'd /we'd like you to start doing, because it will be good for you and what we're trying to do here."

The circumstances will dictate to you if these are questions or requests. If the employee is cooperative, then the buy-in is greater using the questioning method and you can have a more collaborative conversation about what do to differently, and how to do it. If the employee is in denial about the issues or can't think of anything that needs to change or how to make those changes, then you can use the statement method.

Some employees freeze up in coaching meetings and may not be able to consider a wide variety of solutions while sitting in front of you. Other employees are just more stubborn and will be in denial about the issues, or provide you with a string of rationalizations and excuses. For them, you'll need to be firmer and say, "Starting immediately, here's what I want you to Keep on doing; I have no problem with it. Here's what I want you to Stop doing because it's against our policy or not productive, it wastes time, or it interferes with our mission here. And finally, here's what I want you to Start doing because it's necessary and how things need to be done from now on."

The second tool to use for coaching success is called the Three C's and it will remind you of your ability to *Communicate*, *Clarify*, and get the employee to *Commit*. You have to *Communicate* the changes you expect the employee to make in their performance or behavior. You need to *Clarify* the issue and the potential solutions, using examples from the recent past. Finally, you need to get the employee's buy-in and ask her or him to agree to *Commit* to make the changes and how soon. Some coaching issues will require an immediate cessation of their behavior; others will require them to comply over time, once they learn what they need to do.

While each of these three is important, you can probably guess the third is the most important. You can *Communicate* until your breath fails. You can *Clarify* the issue(s) until "it's so clear you can see it if you were standing on the Moon," but if you don't get them to *Commit* to change, none of the work you did with the previous two will have mattered. And the *Commit* piece is not just for today or until the end of the month (when the employee feels the pressure is off or the supervisory oversight has faded); it has to last and that's a request you need to make of the employee as well.

During coaching meetings, some employees will completely agree with what you are asking them to do and you'll leave that discussion thinking you're a genius and the Best HR Person in the World (thereby having earned your right to use that engraved coffee cup someone gave you, probably as a gag gift). The problem comes when you notice that the employee has not changed and the agreed-upon solutions are not being done, or they are being done haphazardly or episodically. Tardiness or other attendance problems are the best examples. You have one or more coaching meetings with employees about being ready to work, be on time, and they agree that because the library doors open at 0900, they need to be on the desk at 0830, not 0905.

After that coaching meeting, which could be Number 1 or Number 12, you see them on time, at the desk, and you are pleased. The next week, they come in late two days in a row and the cycle starts again. You certainly *Communicated* what you want them to do. You certainly *Clarified* both the time to be at work and the importance of being at work with them. The failure is on their part not to *Commit* to the action, now and forever, going forward. And the failure on your part is because you did not request their commitment, by giving them the "Coaching Meeting Closure Speech."

So you ask, "But the employee agreed to come to work on time, ready at the desk. The meeting was short and to the point. What happened?" Of course, the meeting was short and the employee complied with your request to get to work, ready to work, on time. Why? They wanted to get out of the meeting. Some employees will literally say anything to get the heat off, hoping the more and the faster they agree, the faster you will end the discussion.

You can address this by saying, "I hear what you're saying and I appreciate your willingness to agree with what we are talking about. Since I don't want to have this conversation with you more than this time, I need to ask you [here comes the Coaching Meeting Closure Speech], is there any reason, as we sit here today, that you can't come to work on time, and be at the desk by 0830? Are there any obstacles that you see, as we sit here talking today, that will prevent you from complying? If so, let's talk about them now. If not, then I'll expect your full compliance starting [now, later today, next week, next month]."

Some employees are masters at making excuses or rationalizations as to why they are not meeting your performance or behavior expectations. It's easy to get caught in a no-win loop of "Yes, you did" and "No, I didn't" with them, which goes nowhere and can serve to distract you from what's really going on. Hear them out but don't add fuel to the excuse fire. Keep the focus of the conversation on the buy-in, and getting the commitment to change. "I hear what you're saying and that does sound like a challenge with your daycare issues for your son. Let's talk about what I can do or we can do to get you back on track with his." If they continue with more excuses—the same ones said in different ways, or new, creative ones that are not really connected to the main issue—say, "You mentioned that before. Let's get back to the solutions."

The Coaching Meeting Closure Speech is something you need to say and document in your notes. This conversation with your employee is important to do and document because it finalizes the coaching conversation and pins him or her down. It prevents a union or association rep or lawyer from saying that you didn't ask or discuss any underlying circumstances that the employee will try to raise later as a defense. Don't forget to say these same Commitment words every time you have a more formal coaching conversation, especially when you have already had this type of conversation with the employee before.

Always remember: No consequences for the performance or behavior issues and the performance or behavior issues won't change.

COVERING CONFIDENTIALITY

One of the issues that comes up on the employee side with coaching is confidentiality. It's useful to address this during the first coaching meeting you have, especially with new employees to your library. They may have hidden or overt concerns that "what they say will be used in court against them," to quote a suspiciously common phrase in our world. You can address these by saying this: "We may talk about some confidential things. Since you already know I'm not a lawyer, a priest, or a therapist, I can't keep our conversations confidential. If you tell me you're breaking the law or violating our policies,

I'm going to act on that information. I have no choice; I'm not going to cover up or lie for you, or to anyone. If you tell me you're stealing from the library, I will report you. If you tell me you have witnessed violations of our sexual or harassment policies, I'm going to act. But I can give you what I call 'careful confidentiality,' which means if you tell me something like you aren't getting along with or don't like someone who works here, including other bosses, I will keep that between you and me. Make sense?"

KEEPING COACHING FILES

Certain employees are also suspicious when you take notes during coaching meetings. They believe anything you write down will be put into their "Permanent Record" and they will never see it again until it's in a discipline package and it's too late for them to rebut it. You can say, "I may take notes during our meetings. This is to help me remember what we said together. If I do or don't write something down, don't read too much into it." And this is where you can discuss the value of keeping coaching files.

You should keep a physical coaching file on all the employees who work directly for you and/or whom you have coached. This is where you put your evidence of formal coaching discussions, notes that you have taken during these meetings, and any written responses back from the employee (copies of their emails, memos to you, notes they have left for you) about the coaching issues you have been discussing. As you may well know, already being in HR, contrary to mistaken beliefs by other supervisors, a coaching file is not a secondary personnel file. It's not a secret or hidden file you keep on the down-low. It's a way for you to keep track of your after-action coaching reports and meeting recaps.

Every leader, manager, supervisor, or PIC who conducts coaching meetings with their employees (in short, all of them should be coaching early and often) needs to have a hard-copy, physical coaching file, to be added to after every meeting. As I'll discuss in chapter 7 on Performance Evaluations, a well-crafted coaching file just makes it easier to write more effective, thorough, and court-defensible evaluations.

In fact, you should tell every employee they can look at their own coaching file anytime (and no one else's) and add things to it that may not be needed in their actual personnel file—thank-you notes from patrons, classes they took, or any documents they feel will help you or their boss write a thorough performance evaluation on their behalf.

And that's the primary benefit of keeping coaching files; besides reminding us of the coaching conversations we have had over the rating period, it makes it that much easier to write an accurate performance evaluation.

You don't have to have the mind of an elephant, you just have to review the file, which should be kept in date order for your ease of use. Keeping a coaching file for your employees is a fair and accurate way to keep track of their progress. They can review what you have written, so don't put "stupid jerk" on a sticky note and leave it in their file. Be careful what you write down as you document coaching meetings. Stick to the facts—what was said, by who, and what it all means. Don't use labels to describe behaviors. It's not, "He's got a lousy attitude during meetings," it's "Employee Smith needs to participate in staff meetings without being sarcastic or negative." We can coach behaviors better than we can coach labels.

COACHING MEETINGS

Here are some useful ground rules for running coaching meetings:

A goal for each session. This connects to the idea that most coaching meetings should only address one issue at a time. It's not helpful to dump all the employee's perceived sins on to the table with the idea that you need to address each one in a single meeting. It's not a beatdown; it's a coaching conversation, designed to start a change process. You need to prioritize the most important, significant, or urgent concern and focus on that one issue first. Better to have more meetings more often.

Respect for each other's time. Your coaching meetings should start on time and finish somewhere between thirty to ninety minutes. Too short and you may not cover all that needs to be discussed; too long and you run the risk of irritating the employee, who may feel trapped into a long discussion of uncomfortable subjects with you. Keep on track with the points you want to cover and wrap it up with a recap of what you've both agreed upon.

No physical or electronic interruptions. That means no non-urgent phone calls or checking email. Shut the office door and don't allow others to interrupt the discussion. Never commit the mortal sin of looking at email while talking with an employee about issues that affect her or his career success. Conversely, you should make it clear to your employee she or he needs to arrive on time, ready to talk about work, not sneak looks at a smartphone screen.

Completed "homework," readings, or viewings. I put the word "homework" in quotes because it is work that the employee needs to do on work time. Skilled coaches give homework for their coachees to review, study, memorize, or be ready to discuss at the next coaching meeting. For an employee who is late, you can provide a written copy of your attendance policy. You say, "Here you go. Read this before our next meeting and be ready to discuss it fully." Other homework includes templates, cheat sheets, past training handouts, sample reports, or their own reports to review and discuss, articles, websites, and training videos to watch. The list of things you may want them to read, review, study, watch, or download is matched only by the coaching issue. Giving homework also tells your employees that this isn't just a chat about work; it's a meeting that matters and may have consequences later.

Let things percolate. With some employees who have a plethora of issues to address, not only is it not useful to try to solve everything in one long meeting; you will need to let some time pass between meetings. Meeting with the employee on Monday, Wednesday, and Friday is probably two meetings too many. They may need time to think about what you have discussed and time to make the changes you have agreed upon. One meeting per week, discussing the most pressing issue, is usually a good guideline. They and you will need to let time pass, let the discussion sink in, and then go back to work.

Preparation for the next session. Before you wrap up the meeting, remind the employee what was discussed, what was agreed upon in terms of changes or improvements, and then set the stage for the next meeting by talking about homework to be done. Start the next session by asking for a "demonstrated use of the tools." Here, the employee should explain what he or she did differently during the time between the previous meeting and this one. As an example, let's say the previous coaching discussion was about how the employee is not getting along with one of his or her co-workers. You have talked about what to do about that issue. Start the next session by asking how things are going now between the two and what the employee has done differently to try and smooth the waters. Like giving homework, the purpose of asking for a demonstrated use of tools is to see early progress and remind the employee that he or she has a stake in the success of the coaching process.

Running successful coaching meetings may require you to improve your listening skills. We all think we are much better listeners than we really are, especially during difficult conversations. It's often during our harder conversations that we listen most poorly, spending our time thinking about what we want to say and waiting for the other person to stop talking instead of really listening to what he or she is actually saying. Listening well is a whole-brain experience, meaning we should be doing more than just hearing the words. We need to be looking at the other person's body language, hearing his or her tone, "reading between the lines" for what he or she said versus what he or she meant, and doing it all while putting the entire issue—including understanding the past, present, and future—into some kind of context.

USE FEWER YES/NO QUESTIONS

Some managers and supervisors have a habit of asking too many closed-ended questions during coaching discussions. These types of yes/no questions don't usually get much information beyond the affirmative or the negative answers and they don't invite the employee to provide more detail. Perhaps this is a control issue for them, but too many closed-ended questions can put the employee on the defensive and can sound more like an interrogation instead of a discussion.

Some examples:

Closed-ended: "Did you talk to the director about your time card problems?"

Open-ended: "What happened after you spoke with the director about your time card concerns?"

Try to use as many open-ended questions as you can. You're trying to build "conversational momentum" and "open the gates of self-interest," which are two ways of saying you want your employees to feel comfortable enough to start talking about their favorite subject—themselves. Try to limit your use of yes / no questions, except when you want agreement or closure, which is often at the end of the conversation.

There are often three reasons supervisors use a lot of closed-ended questions during coaching meetings: it saves time; they want to exert control over the direction of the conversation; and they are uncomfortable with silence. Some employees go dead quiet, because they are fully considering what you are saying, they don't know how to respond, or they are stressed, anxious, or afraid. Ask your questions and let them answer, no matter how long it takes, and without needing to fill in that conversational space for them.

Coaching Meeting Steps

- Plan for the meeting. (Set the time and place, and provide any handouts or "homework.")
- Open the meeting. (Try to build rapport, then get to the purpose.)
- Describe any problem areas. (Refer to your written talking points; be specific.)
- Help the employee generate solutions. (Try to get the employee's ownership and buy-in; take notes.)
- Handle any excuses, minimizations, rationalizations, denials, or blaming. (Listen fully, then put a fence around each excuse, and get back to the main issue.)
- Discuss the solutions. (Fine-tune the suggested choices.)
- Describe the employee's strengths. (Reward her or his successes.)
- Discuss a development plan. (Prepare for the next session.)
- Close the meeting. (Say thanks and use your notes to provide a verbal and/ or a written or email recap.)

WRAPPING IT ALL UP

Whether your employee will admit it to you or not, the coaching conversation process is a behavioral/performance contract between the two of you. Part of an actual contract calls for "mutual assent," or a "meeting of the minds." You offer suggestions for performance or behavior improvements, or the employee suggests what he or she will do differently (which indicates better buy-in), starting when, and you both agree on that path.

The coaching process should be deadline-driven, results-oriented, and reward-focused, meaning you use praise when you see your employee doing what was discussed and growing into more success with his or her work. The employee owns the solutions, not you.

The coaching contract will not work for an extended period if it is only honored at the point of a sword. Threatening the employee with discipline is not part of the coaching process. Once coaching no longer works—because the employee has failed to see or refused to recognize the sense of shared fate and shared responsibility you have tried to create—then it's time to initiate discipline, as we will discuss in the next chapter.

You are attempting to build "A Spectrum of Influence," where you shift, over time and with effort, into a "Tutorial Role," then more of an "Advisory Role," and then into what can be called "Assisted Discovery."

This last step is where they figure out what to do and how to do it, on their own. Your rising stars/shining stars will get here quickly, often with no more than one meeting or discussion with you. Some of your other employees will—like the dog being told to get off the couch for a solid year—take more time to arrive here. A few of your employees, despite your best intentions—will never get there. Focus your best coaching efforts on those employees where you can get the best results.

Let's get to the next logical step in the HR coaching process—when it no longer works—and then it's time for discipline.

NOTE

1. Peters, Thomas J. and Robert H. Waterman. (1982). *In Search of Excellence: Lessons from America's Best-Run Companies*. Harper & Row.

Chapter 6

Humane and Effective Discipline and Termination Approaches

Your employees are in charge of their own behavior and performance. Some don't realize this until it's too late and they are sitting in front of you at a discipline meeting or are pleading with their union to hire a lawyer to defend them. At those crossroads points, the time for coaching has come and gone.

While many bosses may understand the value and need for a Performance Improvement Plan (PIP) to help address the employee's need to make changes in her or his work efforts—quality of work, meeting deadlines, the need for certain procedural or technical expertise, and so on—my experience suggests they have less comfort using Behavioral Improvement Plans (BIPs) to address so-called deficiencies in the employees "soft skills." These can include: poor and noticeable service attitude when working with co-workers or patrons; complaints from bosses or co-workers about their use of sarcasm, idea killing during staff meetings, rudeness on the phone, anger, negative body language, not participating in team efforts, or even fun stuff, like skipping at-work parties or library staff development activities because they just don't like anyone they work with.

The PIP is for activity-related changes the employee must make; the BIP is for the other 50 percent we hired her or him for—to get along in a work culture with colleagues and patrons and help to create a nourishing and not a toxic work culture.

(In coaching meetings, I have heard angry employees tell me, "I don't have to like anyone here and they don't have to like me. I'm just here to do my job, get paid, and go home." I reply, "That sounds miserable. And you're right. You don't have to like anyone here, but you do have to coexist with everyone here and help your co-workers and bosses when asked. Our patrons don't care if we like each other. But they do expect to be served. We will ask you to do that, if you want to continue working here. As such, here comes your BIP.")

Okay, all of your attempts at coaching an employee, or those tried by the leaders, managers, supervisors, or PICs in your library have been tried and they have failed. Now what? Before we get to the "crossroads" where the next step is progressive discipline, we need to have a Personal Accountability Meeting or a PAM.

USING THE PERSONAL ACCOUNTABILITY MEETING (PAM)

There comes a time in the coaching process when it is really, truly, absolutely up to the employee to make the necessary, required, asked-for changes in his or her performance or behavior. If we define coaching as a series of one or more pre-discipline discussions that seek to make positive changes, then the last coaching meeting is the Personal Accountability Meeting or PAM. The function of this meeting is to tell the employee that you and he or she have reached a crossroads, a decision point. Previous coaching meetings have not seemed to work—the employee either does not make the changes or, more likely, won't sustain them over a span of time. Some employees are masters at seeming to change and then backsliding into old bad habits or work performance deficiencies once they think the boss is not paying attention and the heat is off.

With a PAM, you're having one-on-one meetings with the employees who give you grief and asking them to take ownership of their work performance and behavior. Some old-school HR people call these "Come to Jesus" meetings or "Cards on the Table" meetings, meaning that it is the time and place to ask for accountability and responsibility.

The PAM for work performance issues is used when no amount of discussion, guidance, training or re-training, direct observation, and pointed asking, gets the employee to make the desired changes in the quality of her or his work, meeting deadlines, and doing what is required from the position's actual job duties and descriptions.

The PAM for behavioral issues is useful for concerns like employees who use sarcasm, rudeness to staff or patrons, constant negative opinions, idea killing during staff meetings, or bad body language (eye rolling, heavy sighing, tossing papers aside when given, etc.).

The purpose of the PAM is to put the employee on notice that since you have not seen him or her make or sustain the performance or behavioral changes you've talked about over a (documented) period, then the *next meeting* will not be a coaching discussion; it *will be a discipline discussion*. This usually takes the form of a verbal or written warning. If the employee wants his or her union or association rep after the PAM, that would be the time to set it up.

The key here is not to use the PAM as a threat. Keep your voice neutral and even as you discuss the steps in the PAM. Try explaining your expectations and asking the employee for his or her help. Don't argue or get overly frustrated; tell the employee what he or she needs to do to comply.

Document this conversation, just like you should do for every coaching conversation, and keep it short. The PAM is the last opportunity for the employee to demonstrate compliance. No need to shout, beg, plead, or threaten the employee with consequences beyond just the next reasonable step in the discipline process. He or she should know, by the end of the PAM, that the time for talking is coming to an end.

I've used the phrase "crossroads conversation" to define the PAM because it's all about the choices you need to make as an HR leader (to continue on to the next disciplinary step, if necessary) and the choices the employee needs to make if he or she wants to stop the coaching process (by being better at his or her job).

Consider that the keyword in the phrase Personal Accountability Meeting is "Accountability." This should mean that the employee either takes ownership, at some point in the coaching process, and makes the changes to his or her behavior or performance, or you do what you need to do and initiate discipline. The challenge, of course, is the word "accountability" is subject to interpretation by the employee. He or she may think, "I come to work mostly on time. Why is my boss making such a big deal if I'm a few minutes late?" Taking real accountability means he or she should say, "I need to be at work on time, ready to do my job. From now on, this is what I will do." The good news is that sometimes this happens, as a result of your coaching efforts. The bad news is that it may not stick or the employee will continue to feel resentful toward you and the library because you are "forcing me to comply with stupid policies or outdated rules."

The purpose of the PAM is to communicate the issues you're concerned about, clarify the solutions you expect, and get their commitment to change, starting now. The PAM is a serious discussion, often initiated at a time when you're frustrated. Consider having this important meeting sooner, before the employee hardens his or her position about you in your HR leadership role.

The goal of the PAM is to explain your next move to the employee and ask for compliance. You aren't "threatening him or her with discipline," and the meeting shouldn't deteriorate into that territory. Stay professional, recap what you have said in an email to the employee, and see where the next steps take you both. At this point, whether or not they receive some form of discipline (or even get fired) is up to them.

DEFINING PROGRESSIVE DISCIPLINE

For the most part, there are seven ways an employee, at any level in the organization, can be fired: (1) violation of departmental policies and procedures; (2) work performance; (3) attendance; (4) poor service attitude; (5) conflict with others; (6) gross misconduct; and (7) dishonesty or lying.

To me, it feels like the concept and operational approach to "Progressive Discipline" has developed a bad reputation over recent years. I hear HR people say they don't use it that way, or they're hesitant to use it with civil service employees, as opposed to at-will employees. Or their union rules prevent them from using it, or they have somehow modified it to fit the current legal necessity, where it seems like we can no longer tell employees what we want them to do differently, warn them—verbally and later in writing—or demote, transfer, suspend, or terminate them, even with cause.

These are often the same HR people who tell me they can't have a "coaching conversation" with an employee in a union environment because it is (mis)perceived as "discipline" and therefore the employee is immediately entitled to a rep. As I discussed in chapter 5 on the need for and the approach to employee coaching, library leaders, managers, and supervisors should be able to speak to their people about any work-related performance or behavior-based issue, without fear.

Even in organizations—and many libraries are not unionized—there seems to be a belief that any coaching or corrective discussion is somehow discipline-related, even if the manager or supervisor never mentions that word. As I have said then and now, once you say to an employee, "If I do not see the specific changes (not just 'be better') I'm asking you to make, the next conversation you and I have about this issue will include discipline as a consequence." This foreshadows the last-chance, last-step coaching conversation known as the "Personal Accountability Meeting" or the PAM I just described above.

Can you skip steps in the discipline process? True progressive discipline is a flexible process, not a carved-in-stone set of edicts. While I'm not a labor law attorney, my short answer is, "Of course! You may have to, if the behavior or performance issue is egregious." We would never say, "Now, Jerry, you've been caught stealing from the library petty cash drawer three times. We'd like you to steal a little less each week for the next three weeks." We would move to suspend Jerry, conduct an investigation as to the length and depth of his theft problem, and make an informed decision as to his termination.

I define progressive discipline as "discipline that increases in intensity and consequences: coaching meetings; verbal warnings; written warning(s); demotion, duties removed, hours changed, salary changed, transfer to another branch (often done in harassment or bullying cases); suspension; and termination."

When we consider terminating an employee, it's easy to get caught up in the Hollywood or TV moment that requires you to say, "You're fired!" In best practice, it is a measured process that is not driven by the emotions of the HR department or the employee's direct boss, but by following a series of steps, which are well-documented in our written HR-related policies and procedures. Whether they memorize them or not, every employee should know (or at least be exposed to them)—as a result of their new-hire orientations, the onboarding process, and continuous updates—the HR response to discipline. Just as we reward great work performances and a team-success attitude, we address the opposite, first with coaching (the first, best opportunity for the employee to correct) and then with discipline (the next, and possibly the last opportunity, for the employee to correct).

In my former state, California, civil service employees in jeopardy of formal discipline or pending termination are entitled to a formal meeting with the HR director or their designees, otherwise known as a "Skelly Hearing." The elements of a California "Skelly Hearing" include:

- The employee must receive notice of the proposed discipline (aka Notice of Adverse Action, or "Notice");
- Notice must identify the specific rule/policy that has allegedly been violated by the employee;
- Notice must allege a factual basis for the violation ("the cause for discipline");
- Notice must be served with all documents that were relied upon by the official proposing the discipline;
- Notice must provide a deadline for any response;
- Notice must include the effective date of the discipline.

Your state may have a similar process for civil service employees versus at-will employees; you must know yours, inside and out.

PROBATIONARY PERIOD DECISIONS

I'm a huge fan of the probation process in organizations. Some bosses (and even employees) see it as a one-way street, where the decision to cut the employee loose at the end of the period is solely at the discretion of HR. It's not. Just as the organization can say, "For a variety of reasons, it's not working out and we are going to wish you luck in your future endeavors," the employee can choose to leave before or right up to the end of the probation period, for reasons she or he shares or doesn't. It is, in reality, a two-way street.

For probationary periods to work, they need: concrete deadlines (ninety days, six months, or one year are common time periods); to be strictly enforced (no extensions to probation periods for behavior reasons, only training gaps, which must be rectified and demonstrated as successful); and to be fair to all employees (no favoritism or allowing a fifth or sixth chance to improve).

I view probation periods like a long-term blind date: prove to me I made the right choice in selecting you. Demonstrate the kind of behaviors that justify why I'm spending my time, money, and energy on you. And if you don't like it here, you can go, with no hard feelings.

In my consulting and HR coaching experience, organizations benefit from a "no mercy" rule when it comes to extending probationary periods. This means they don't do it. If there is doubt in the HR office or among the new employee's bosses (and even with her or his peers), as to whether the person needs an extension, the answer is a hard and swift "no" and we don't allow this person to stay.

If you have worked in civil service organizations for even the briefest of moments, especially in an HR role, you have certainly heard a variation of this conversation: "We should have never let Phil go past probation. You know our city/county; it's almost impossible to get rid of a bad employee once they pass probation. We should have said no three months ago and now it's too late. Nobody can stand the guy and we are stuck with him."

First, I disagree with the assumption that "nothing can be done" with a problematic employee once the probationary period has passed. Of course, we will use documentation, several attempts at coaching, and the fair and legal use of progressive discipline, up to and including termination. It just takes effort, and that's why some bosses and even some well-meaning HR people don't want to do it. The hard work necessary to legally separate the non-performing employee should never be seen as an insurmountable obstacle.

Second, extending probation to an employee who does not seem to want to work hard or fit into the nourishing work culture we all want to create should not be "rewarded" with a continuation of the job. When we do this—because we don't want to have the "thanks and goodbye" meeting—guess what this says to the other employees? "Hard work, cooperation, and collaboration don't matter here." They become resentful of the employee who slacks and even more resentful of both HR and the library leaders, managers, and supervisors who failed to do the right thing, early enough.

Employees who are toxic or act as deadwood don't just harm themselves; they injure the workforce. Good employees quit instead of waiting for HR and management to get rid of problematic co-workers. People who stay turn miserable, seeing that the employee who should never have been given the chance to stay is still there, day after day, after month, after year.

Want proof? After a bad employee leaves, her or his now-former co-workers will come up to you and say, "Thank God! We were waiting for her or him to go! What took so long?" When these disruptive employees finally quit on their own (or get properly fired when HR steps up and does its job correctly), they have what I call the "Two-Person Retirement Party." This consists of the employee and someone from HR in a room alone, collecting ID badges, facility keys, and being handed a final check. No one else cares she or he is going out the door forever and in fact, they are hugely relieved. Contrast that version with an employee who worked hard, got along with everyone, and was widely beloved. When she or he leaves or retires we have to rent out a meeting hall for all the people who want to come by and say farewell, give hugs, and eat cake.

If a new employee is approaching the end of her or his probationary period and is working and getting along fine with all, but is still not understanding the technical complexities of the job, extend the period and get this person trained. If there are any doubts for other reasons, then don't. The misery you save for yourself and others will be well noted.

DISCIPLINING OUR FORMER PEERS: A TOUGH TEST

One familiar topic of conversation for many new supervisors in multi-day leadership workshops is a dicey one: How do you effectively supervise, coach, and discipline employees who used to be your peers? This discussion often takes place early in these programs, when the instructor is asking the participants to voice their biggest challenges and what they want to get from the training experience. This is an issue you, as an HR professional, must address with your newest managers or supervisors.

Here's what you can say to them to help them handle this change in their organizational status:

Giving orders or enforcing policies is never easy on a good day. Disciplining people you have known for years, came on the job with, or have socialized with outside of work is tough to do. You may be able to flip that switch, once you become a leader, manager, supervisor, or PIC, but they may or may not be able to make the transition in their minds.

Supervising and disciplining your former peers can put them at either end of a spectrum. On the one end, you have your ol' buddy, who thinks, "Great! My pal is now in charge! I don't have to work as hard as before. He or she is gonna cut me some major slack and we can hang out and kick back, just like the good old days. Life is suddenly good."

On the other end, you may have an employee who never was your friend, who thinks, "Great! I can't stand this jerk and now he/she is my boss! I'm not gonna listen to one word. I'm doing my own thing. I should have gotten that promotion. Life suddenly sucks."

This puts the new supervisor in an immediate bind. "How do I keep my old friendships intact and get the employees who do and don't like me to do their work?" The truth is, you may not be able to keep your old friendships intact and you may never win over the person who cannot stand you now and never really liked you before you became their boss. The answer starts with an early conversation, alone and with both types of employees, customized for their ears.

An example of the discussions, first with the employee who thinks he or she is on Easy Street:

To your friend, it should come out something like this: "You and I go back a long way and we started on this job together. I appreciate your friendship and I value your experience and your job skills. I have new responsibilities now and I don't want them to ruin our relationship. I have people watching over me who expect results, so I want to be able to count on you to do your job just as well as before. I'm going to have different boundaries with you as your boss. I know you won't expect me to play favorites. I'm in a different role now and as your boss, I have certain expectations about you getting your work done at the quality this organization expects. I'm asking you to take my orders seriously and do your job. I'm hoping you will continue to be one of my top people."

To the employee who is not a fan, it should come out something like this: "I notice every time I ask you to complete an assignment in front of the rest of the team, you sigh, roll your eyes, throw down your pen, and act like I'm asking you to do something that's outside the scope of your job. I realize you and I have never been close friends and that's okay. I'm asking you to put your personal feelings aside and do what I've asked you to do. I realize you wanted this position too and that I got it. We may not have been friends before; however, I have always respected your work experience and job skills. I have new responsibilities now and I'd like to be able to count on your help and your experience and knowledge, just as before. I'm hoping you will become one of my top people."

Same melody, different verses. Waiting to have this conversation after problems arise, from misplaced expectations of favoritism from your pal or angry apathy from your not-a-pal, means it's too late to get off on the right foot. It's important to address these potentially difficult behavioral issues, from each end of the peer spectrum, as soon as you are in your new role.

USING TIME STUDIES

It's certainly possible that some of your younger employees, or those who have never had a full-time job in a government organization, may have a time usage issue. (It's not a "time management problem" because they are not actually managing their time; they're misusing it, on our dime.) They seem to spend more time looking at their smartphones, chatting with patrons or co-workers, or being invisible when you go to look for them at their desks. In the worst cases, they go for long spans without doing the work they are being paid to do.

One short-term tool is your use of a time study with them. Here is what you say, as part of a coaching meeting:

> I've noticed you don't seem to be at your desk when I look for you. I'm getting complaints from patrons and even some of your co-workers that you aren't available to help when things get busy. I'd like you to start actually measuring your time and your efforts, in your work day. As such, I'm going to give you this tool. Take these log forms and account for your time, in thirty-minute increments, for your entire library shift. For example, when you leave your desk today at 11:30 to go to lunch and you return at 12:30, you'll simply note one hour in your log. This timesheet should be accompanied by proof of your efforts, so if you spent from 1:00 to 3:00 working on a weeding or shelving project, note where you did that work in the library. Give this to me personally, every day at 5:30, and I'll go over it with you briefly.

At first glance, this tool may seem punitive, and even childish, but it does make the employee account accurately for his or her time in thirty-minute chunks, all shift long. Big law firms ask their most seasoned attorneys to do this every day, so they can bill at their usual astronomical hourly rates. No need to call the employee's union or association for permission; it's not discipline. You're using it as a coaching tool, not for seasoned employees who may be having a rough couple of weeks, but for those employees who have made it clear that they are manipulating the system and the good faith of the organization by not giving us an honest day's work.

Employees who gripe about having to fill out these accountability sheets can quickly free themselves from this activity by demonstrating that they are truly hard at work on your behalf, and that they don't disappear for hours without a valid reason.

Two weeks seems to be a reasonable time for you to measure the employee's outputs and for the employee to be able to show what he or she does to earn his or her pay.

HELPING YOUR COLLECTION OF BOSSES HANDLE
HARD HR CONVERSATIONS

It's important to remind your leaders, managers, supervisors, and PICs that no matter how tough or stressful these meetings seem for you as the bosses (especially at the end of the behavioral spectrum: discipline and termination), they are doubly difficult for the employees. They realize these sessions have much more tension or urgency attached to them because you hold the power of their promotion, pay, duties, responsibilities, or even their continued employment, in your hands.

As a result, there are three possibilities for the more difficult meetings: the employee will sit sullenly and pout through the session, only agreeing to some points and not others; the employee will debate, argue, and challenge every point, raising the emotional temperature in general and your blood pressure in particular; or the employee will nod and agree and say, "You're absolutely right. I need to do that and I will." For this last type, the meeting ends and you think to yourself, "I'm a genius. I'm the best HR leader on the planet," only to discover later (after no change is evident) that the employee simply agreed with you just to get out of the room as quickly as possible.

Having conducted or attended a number of these high-stress or even high-risk meetings, I know that a sticking point for most supervisors happens at the point during the meeting when the employee simply refuses to acknowledge the presenting problem. This can lead to conversations we all used to have in the schoolyard:

> *You:* "After reviewing your attendance records, I wanted to speak to you about getting to work on time."
>
> *Hostile Employee:* "I don't have an attendance problem."
>
> *You:* "Do so."
>
> *Hostile Employee:* "Do not."
>
> *You:* "Do so." And so on, and so on, and so on.

There are four keys to help prevent this circular dead-end conversation:

Always focus on behaviors, not labels. Don't say, "You're always late," which is a label. Discuss the late-arriving or poor attendance-related behaviors; for example, "On Monday you were fifteen minutes late. On Tuesday you were thirty minutes late." Don't say, "You're not a good team player," which is a label. Say, "I've noticed that when it gets busy, you don't help your co-workers with the group projects and deadlines you're all responsible for."

Always speak from a position of proof, either data or direct observation, rather than from speculation or guessing. Provide copies of your HR policies that spell out the right ways to work here. The proof lies in the numbers, or what my father, Dr. Karl Albrecht, calls, "the intra-ocular impact test," that is, what hits you between the eyes. Pull the attendance rosters; pull the email copies where the employee promised something and didn't deliver; and pull documents that support your discussion. And direct observation means something you saw, or that was reported to you by a reliable source (peer manager, your boss, a trusted subordinate with no hidden agenda against the employee).

Always keep moving on with the meeting, even if the employee refuses to see there is a behavioral or performance issue. I've seen supervisors play the "did not–did so" game for twenty minutes. I've seen managers and supervisors either unwilling or unable to move forward until the employee finally agrees, "Yes, you're right. I am late all the time! Okay? Satisfied now?" If the employee refuses to see the issue from your perspective, save yourself the aggravation by saying, "I'm sorry you don't agree. I feel it is an important issue and as your supervisor or this library's HR director/manager, I'm going to ask you to stop the behavior and fix the problem."

Always return the focus back to employee. How do you answer, "How come you never talk to Kate about her attendance problems? She's late a lot too. Why are you always picking on me about coming in a few minutes late?" With this: "I'm not picking on you and I will address Kate's issues as well. We're talking about you, not her, so let's go back to what we were discussing." Put a fence around the employee's excuses, rationalizations, or blaming and go back to getting her or his buy-in on fixing the issue.

Some libraries take most of the power to solve their subordinates' problems, by telling them to speak to HR before they do anything related to investigating, solving, or stopping employee behavioral problems. Other libraries take a more hands-off approach, empowering their leaders to confront and manage their own issues, and only come to HR for guidance when the issue exceeds their experience, expertise, or authority. From a training perspective, it will help you greatly to know which is which where you are working. Otherwise, you could spend a lot of time teaching managers and supervisors to do things their HR department does not want them to touch under most circumstances.

As an example, some libraries ask their managers and supervisors to contact HR immediately if one of their people makes a sexual harassment complaint. At that point, HR will take over completely, interview the parties, review past documentation and any existing evidence, and make a decision as to any discipline, victim support, punitive or group training, and so forth.

In this same situation, other libraries ask their managers and supervisors to handle the claim themselves, investigating the issues, interviewing the parties, even suggesting the appropriate discipline, if any, and, as one HR director puts it, "bring the whole case to us with a nice bow on top and let us have it from there."

While I understand the need for the first approach, we want our managers and supervisors to do the right thing, get expert HR/labor law guidance right away, and let those who know the library policies best handle it legally and effectively. On the other hand, I also see the need to let bosses be bosses and not have to run to HR every time there is a minor-issue blip on their departmental radar screen. This approach teaches managers and supervisors to defer, not trust their instincts and experience, and wait for HR to ride to the rescue. This process does not work as the organization grows and HR gets too busy to respond immediately. A backlog of more serious cases (sexual harassment, workplace violence, threats, discrimination, etc.), where HR is slow in responding, is bad for everybody's business.

Here are four core "macros" to help you train your library leaders, managers, supervisors, and PICs on HR subjects. Use these as primary discussion points as to how and why we involve ourselves in employees' behavior and performance issues, good and bad:

"Firm, fair, and consistent." This is more than just a slogan; it should become an operating style for the HR department and all managers and supervisors. This approach—these words—is what every employee expects, wants, and demands from their bosses and the library. These terms, and the consistency that they are supposed to represent, have a history in the labor union movement. This is how the unions expect management to treat their members. This is the language new and longtime managers and supervisors can use in group and individual coaching meetings, to set their standards for performance and behavior; for example, "My approach is to treat every employee the same: firmly, fairly, and consistently. This will give you a better idea of what I expect from you and what you can expect from me."

"Business impact." This is a great phrase to use for those difficult performance evaluations, coaching meetings, discipline sessions, or even termination meetings. This concept says to all employees, "We will get involved, with a coaching, discipline, or termination response, when what you do *impacts the business* of this department or our library in a negative way. Conversely, we will provide rewards, recognition, pay raises, and promotions when what you do *impacts the business* in a positive way." This phrase is also quite useful in those testy meetings, where the employee shouts, "You're just saying these things because you don't like me. In fact, you've never liked me!" As a supervisor, a good response is, "No. This problem has nothing to do with my personal feelings toward you. It's a business impact issue. What you have been doing—showing up late, taking and making personal calls throughout the day—hurts the business of this department and our library. When other people have to cover your work and do theirs, it hurts our business."

"Consequence behavior." Another great phrase to use in individual and group meetings to set early standards or explain why you must take certain HR or discipline-related actions. If the employees don't think that consequences exist, then they will continue their negative behavior unabated. The message from HR and the managers and supervisors should be: "There are consequences for these behaviors. When you do them, when you violate our policies, you can expect to bear the consequences, up to and including discipline or termination."

POV. Sometimes, it's hard for longtime managers and supervisors to forget what it was like to be a new, struggling, or anxious employee. Sometimes, it helps the boss to put herself or himself into the shoes of the employee and see things from her or his *point of view*. This is useful in answering the "why" question for certain employee behaviors or performance problems. Is it an off-the-job issue? Is the employee angry at someone or me? Do they need more support, different duties, or a job change? It helps the managers and supervisors to try and live in their employees' world and see things from her or his perspective, if just for a moment, to help clarify the possible reasons, the next steps, or the most effective response.

HAVING THE "CROSSROADS" CONVERSATION WITH SOON-TO-BE-TERMINATED EMPLOYEES

As a lifelong baseball fan, I enjoy most baseball-themed movies. In *Moneyball*, the 2011 movie based on the 2003 book by Michael Lewis, Brad Pitt plays real-life Oakland A's general manager, Billy Beane. He teams with Jonah Hill's character, Peter Brand (based on the real baseball/football stats guru, Paul DePodesta), to remake his struggling and cash-poor team.

Two pivotal scenes show the difficulty of giving someone who works for you bad news. In the first scene, Beane tells Brand to go to a player and tell him he has been traded. Trying to be empathetic, Brand goes into a long explanation as to why the club had to make the decision and tries to put a somewhat positive spin on it. The conversation ends in a disaster, with an angry player and a flustered team executive.

Beane tells Brand he is giving the player way too much information and trying to rationalize the decision. He needs to be more direct and to the point. In the subsequent scene, Brand has to speak with another player who has been traded and tells him that news, gives him the contact phone number for the traveling secretary at the new baseball club, and wishes him well. That's it. No need for a long discussion, especially since it won't change the decision.

In my long career as a workplace violence prevention consultant, I have had to be in the room with HR as they fired someone, or done it on their behalf. These are not pleasant conversations, with angry people who have already made threats or hurt people, and now realize they are on the way out. I have often used the phrase, "We came to a crossroads, where we had to make a hard business decision. We are going to let you go. I realize it's easy to take it personally, but it was really not about that. We came to a point where we had to make a business decision."

These conversations are never easy and don't always go as predicted. I have found the "crossroads" theme can help the HR professional explain what happened, without having to overexplain. My sense, too, is this approach may give the departing employee a face-saving way to rationalize what happened as somehow "not my fault."

WHEN IT'S TERMINATION TIME

This final meeting is not a negotiation. The HR decision has been made and nothing the employee says should change that. It's not a long-winded meeting or a rehash of their past sins. I usually use the phrase, "We've had to make a business decision and we've decided to let you go from your employment here."

My experience has shown me that once an employee suddenly and finally realizes he or she is being fired for performance or behavior reasons, their *primary* concern is getting another job, followed by getting whatever final monies they are owed. Their *primary fear* is that you and/or the organization will provide a negative reference for them. Because this is their ultimate distraction, they may not hear or listen to anything you or the HR people say during the meeting, in terms of last paychecks, continuing benefits, vacation hours, and so on.

Therefore, you must decide on the reference question strategy *prior* to a termination meeting. I often provide the employee with an absolutely generic "verification" letter (which is not a reference letter in reality) that simply provides any prospective employer the former employee's name, date of hire, date of separation, duties, and/or last pay grade. This does not harm the library organization in any way; it simply verifies what the former employee will be putting on their résumés or applications and mirrors what we would say if the employer called HR to verify the facts.

One of your most empathetic HR tools for your termination toolkit is a concept known as "Benevolent Severance." Here, the employee who is being let go is given something to physically hold before she or he departs. Unless the person decides to storm out of the building, in which case, it doesn't matter what we say or do, the purpose of Benevolent Severance is to use the last meeting as a way to create a soft landing for the person. We do this to show compassion, even during a difficult conversation, and as a way to smooth the transition from working here to suddenly not.

Your Benevolent Severance package could include things like:

- resigning in lieu of termination;
- uncontested unemployment claim;
- a continuation of EAP services for three months;
- paying their medical benefits for an additional thirty days;
- providing a "here's when you worked here and what you did" letter (not a recommendation/reference, but a verification device);
- thirty days of an outplacement service;
- quick access to vacation pay or retirement account funds.

I have had this argument with library board attorneys or other lawyers attached to the HR process, that somehow this is "rewarding" the employee for being problematic, difficult, and tedious. "Why are we giving her or him these things? We need to be done with them!"

I disagree. Even people who hate their jobs, hate their bosses, and hate their co-workers don't usually want to get fired. (Ironic, right?) This approach of giving them something to walk out with shows them empathy in a difficult time.

Chapter 7

Performance Evaluations
Fair, Legal, Honest, and Accurate

When it comes to the value and necessity of conducting regular performance evaluations, if an employee is shocked, surprised, saddened, or outraged by his or her work performance scores or the comments and feedback in the PE document, we have not done professional jobs as managers and supervisors and as supportive HR providers. We have certainly not used coaching meetings to support and guide the employee over the rating period.

Good bosses provide feedback, through daily coaching conversations, frequent or necessary discussions about an employee's performance or behavior, and through the more formal performance evaluation process. What's that you say? Your library bosses at every level don't like doing employee evaluations (or worse, don't do them at all)? This needs to change and this chapter will help you help them to either start doing them or improve upon them.

All employees have the right to know how they are doing in their jobs, what they need to do differently, and how, if they so choose, to move to the next level in the organization. This written, discussed, and archived performance evaluation document helps with all of those and more. It serves as a historical record, a coaching subject referral, and both a goal-setting and a goal-achieving step-by-step plan. It tells your employees what they need to *Keep* doing (because it's working well and it's good for our patrons and our co-workers); *Stop* doing (because it's against policy, a waste of time, or non-value-added activities); and *Start* doing (because it will help the employee work faster, smarter, easier, and be better for the library as a whole).

Let's get back to talking about the value of doing regular (annual, biannual, or even quarterly) performance evaluations. Your employees can't fix what they don't know about and we have a duty of care to the organization and to our employees to provide honest feedback, praise, and notice of what needs correcting.

And let's define supervisors or above as those who are designated by their own job duties to do performance evaluations. These employees should be designed as having supervisory and/or managerial power over their subordinates, having authority to assign job duties and tasks, set their work schedules, use coaching and progressive discipline, and therefore, be in a position of authority to evaluate their work. As an example, if your library designates PICs as supervisors, then they should evaluate the people who work for them. But if your PICs are more like "leads" (or what a construction site would call a "foreperson") and they are only in charge of that particular work shift and its obstacles and outcomes, and the evals are done by their bosses, then they are not, by that definition, a "supervisor."

THE WHYS OF PERFORMANCE EVALUATIONS

Performance evaluations provide us with a formal attempt to measure the multiple intersections between our employees' work performance (the specific knowledge, skills, and abilities [KSAs] they bring to their jobs) and our library or city/county's strategic plan; how they demonstrate they can follow our policies, use appropriate behaviors in our workplace, and work effectively in a team. We ask our leaders to look at their employees' actual behaviors versus the desired behaviors we want for all of them, and see how close they came. The PE conversation should be yet another version of a regular coaching conversation, between the library leader and the employee, albeit a more formal one.

Let's look at the value of the process and why it needs to be a focal point in every library's HR department. PEs should:

- Be a written, factual, timely, discussed, confidential, and historical document, created with courage, honesty, and care, that trails the employee in her or his personnel file, through their employment with us.
- Reward employees for their good work, efforts, attitude, and accomplishments, and let them know where they stand with the organization and their bosses.
- Help HR and managers and supervisors to effectively match their employees' job duties, descriptions, and requirements to actual (observed) work done.
- Tell the employees specifically what they need to do to improve.
- Identify job skills gaps that will require more or updated training.
- Help them set their own professional and educational goals.

- Help employees set and meet their career objectives, if they want to promote or move into other supervisory, managerial, or leadership positions.
- Emphasize the importance of working successfully in teams, to meet interdepartmental and organizational goals.
- Be a coaching tool, not just on the day of the PE meeting, but going forward.
- Offer a standardized method of evaluation, used across the organization, to make it fair, communicated, and achievable.
- Help HR and/or managers and supervisors to create reasonable, well-designed, and fair Performance Improvement Plans (PIPs) and Behavioral Improvement Plans (BIPs).
- Serve as notice to the employee that she or he needs to improve, as it is a justification for progressive discipline.
- Help HR and the organization make fair and legal promotions.
- Be connected to the library or the city/county's strategic plan.
- Serve as a strategic planning tool, especially for HR decisions about staffing up or down, hiring, restructuring or combining jobs, and benchmarking.
- Assist HR and library leaders with succession planning efforts.

OUR FORMS AND FUNCTIONS

In my perfect HR world, we would encourage our library organizations to do PEs more than annually. Follow my logic here:

When I was a supervisor for the city of San Diego, we did our evals annually, on the anniversary date of the employee's hiring. This meant when I had fifteen employees working for me, I did them all year long, which was tedious because it was hard to keep track of when and who. Then the city switched and we did PEs every December, which was tedious because of the holidays, and the end of the year was always a stressful work period, and we all had to cram them all in before December 31.

Then, in a rare stroke of genius, the city said, "We will evaluate our employees not annually, but quarterly." And we all howled to the heavens that this was unfair and time-consuming and a horrible burden on us as supervisors and managers. But they were exactly right. Doing evals every quarter made for a shorter format, a briefer meeting with the employee, more versus less "customer closeness" with our employees (seeing them work and interacting about it, more coaching, more often), and an easier recap of their overall efforts in a final PE done at the end of the year (Month 1+ Month 4+ Month 8 = The Summary, completed in Month 12).

I've never been a huge fan of the annual performance evaluation because it's often done wrong by managers and supervisors who find the process onerous, don't fill out the form correctly (and part of that is because it's designed poorly), blow through the face-to-face meeting with the employee (or worse, don't meet with them at all and just ask them to sign the document without a discussion), and then call it good for the year. Why should we ask employees to care about this process if their bosses don't?

And I have seen so many HR professionals and the organization's managers and supervisors chafe under the PE process because they hate the form. Change it. Get a committee of your library leaders together, ask for their specific input, and make it better. Steal the design and language from good ones from other organizations and make them your own. There is no valid reason to stick with a PE form design that has never been liked or effective, just because "that's the way we've always done it."

Back to my perfect HR world, I would prefer to see a PE form with just three levels of measurement, not twenty-three. I see way too many forms with markers like "Outstanding," "Exceptional," and "Mostly Unsatisfactory," as if we could ever accurately define those characteristics in an employee. I would prefer to see Above Standard (with justification as to why), Standard (as in, "Thank you for doing the job just as we hired you to do it"), and Below Standard (with specific examples of the deficiencies, not labels, and an accompanying Performance Improvement Plan—PIP).

Still, even with this three-choice format, problems can arise. Some managers and supervisors will always tend to choose the middle box and give everyone a "Standard" rating because they don't want to do the necessary documentation work for the Below Standard employee, often because it will reflect poorly on them as not having done enough (or any) coaching over the rating period.

Further, employees will compare each other's evaluations and go screaming into your office (either literally or at a speedy clip) to tell you their boss got it oh-so-wrong when comparing their work efforts to their colleagues'. This is why you need to help your library's leaders set the tone with all employees, if you decide to use this three-choice form. Your language to them should say, "The Performance Evaluation process is not a popularity contest. It is designed to be a fair example of how we judge both work performance and work behavior. Your bosses are entitled to their opinions as to the quality of your work. We will ask them to give us examples of when you have worked above the standard that we hired you for and we will ask them for examples when you have not worked to the level of your job duties and descriptions. Please do not mistake the Standard evaluation as some sort of denigration of your efforts. It means you're doing what we ask you to do and we appreciate it. If you receive a Below Standard evaluation, it will include a Performance Improvement Plan, which your boss has discussed with HR and had it approved. You have the right to prepare a rebuttal of your performance evaluation and if your boss or HR has made factual errors in the document, we will correct those and reissue it. However, since the quality of both your work performance and work behaviors are the opinion of your bosses, it is not subject to change if you disagree with their assessment." (In other words, if you don't like what you got, work harder and/or behave better during the next rating period.)

It's hard to know if most frontline employees realize they can rebut their performance evaluations and/or review their personnel files, with notice. If they do, they often don't understand the process or the fact that rebutting a performance evaluation form they disagree with does not mean the supervisor has to change his or her conclusions, unless there was a significant factual error.

I think the same rule applies when employees are so angry about some formal reprimand or evaluation they have received from HR or their supervisors that they think refusing to sign the document somehow changes things. We need to say to them, "I understand your frustration or that you don't agree with the need for this document. It's your choice not to sign it. It won't change the fact that I gave it to you. I'll note your refusal to sign it in your file. However, even though you didn't sign it, you're still responsible for making the performance or behavioral changes documented here."

This dissatisfaction with the PE process at both the boss and employee levels can come when both feel it's a waste of time because the library employee "has already reached the top step, can't promote to a higher level, or get any more money, so what's the point of doing them?" This is unfair to the employee, even if it's true and she or he cannot move up or earn more pay. Employees have the right to know how they are doing, even if not everyone wants to get feedback. And bosses have a duty of care to support their people and ask for compliance in work performance and work behavior. Even if the employee says she or he doesn't care about a PE and doesn't want the meeting, too bad, her or his supervisor must do it anyway, for the benefit of both of them and the organization.

From an HR perspective, demand your directors, managers, and supervisors do more than just check boxes and scratch out a few words of praise prose, or worse, scrawl noncommittal nothings in the narrative sections. Remind them that quality-crafted evals are an important part of your job and theirs. Further, that they can and should use the completed PE form as an ongoing coaching tool with their employees. It doesn't have to be a "one and done" document; it can trail the employee all the way up until the next one is written. Using the PE as a reference helps to keep the employee on track with the original improvement plans. We need to change the thinking about PEs from being an annual or semiannual process to a useful supervisory, coaching, and oversight tool.

The PE form needs to go into the employee's file, every year. It is an HR-driven, historical, legal, guiding, trailing document that serves the interest of the organization and the employee. I have told employees, "Make a copy of your eval each time. If you plan to leave this organization at some point, take the most recent one with you and show it to your interviewer at the next job you go to. You have the right to this document; it's all about you." (Of course, this is only useful advice if the PE is not Below Standard.)

And speaking of Below Standard evals, how many is enough? I have seen HR organizations allow an employee to collect years (and even decades of poor evals) with no apparent consequence. How can this be allowed to happen? What is the message to the employee: Not good is good enough for us? Keep on being mediocre at your job, largely because neither your boss nor HR have the courage to demand better? How about once, and then we help this employee's boss enforce the PIP, and if we see no positive changes by the next rating period, we let the employee go? (Another reason to have an annual collection of PEs in the employee's file is to provide proof that we made hard but legal and necessary business decisions on behalf of the organization. This is especially true when we are reviewing the evals of probationary employees at that important go or no-go period.)

PAST PE PROBLEMS: TIMES AND TIMING

There are some issues that come to mind when it comes to PEs and a critical one is timing. Should the supervisor give the PE form to her or his employee before the PE meeting or wait and give it to the employee (or more likely, spring it on them) during the meeting and allow the employee time to review it during the meeting? Some bosses argue that if they give their employees the completed form too early, they will overly critique it, compare theirs with their colleagues, and possibly come into the meeting upset. But if we wait and give it to them during the meeting, and not provide enough time to read it fully and digest the conclusions, then they will be flustered and possibly upset then too. (I'll discuss how to handle various employee reactions during PE meetings later in this chapter.)

I always suggest a sweet spot, where the boss gives it to her or his employee a few days before the meeting and says, "This is what we will go over when we meet. Read it over and make any notes for the points you want to discuss. Please don't share it with your colleagues, since I have asked all of them to do the same."

Another timing issue is one that I don't have a perfect answer for. I call it the "car accident" dilemma. Let's say one of your employees is driving a city/county car on behalf of the library and she or he gets in an accident while on duty and it's her or his fault. The employee received a written warning for the accident, which went into her or his personnel file. This accident happened in February. In December (if you're only doing my not-my-first-choice annual-only evals) when you fill out the form and come to the section on "Driving Ability" (if that's a category), how do you score the employee, Standard or Below Standard? Some bosses say, "Standard, because they had the accident and did not get into another during the rating period, so they're fine." Other bosses say, "Below Standard. The accident happened during the rating period and it must be noted. The fact that they didn't get into another one is good, but that's expected." I agree with the latter approach, although I have seen HR people agree with the former.

PE TRAPS, PITFALLS, AND BIASES

Should you use the PE from a previous supervisor? This can be both a lazy trap and an ethical problem. The lazy trap is when the new supervisor takes a "cut and paste the same language" approach to the new eval. Ethical problems arise when perhaps the former boss did not write a very good eval, had a less-than-positive but inaccurate portrayal of the employee, or wrote a glowing one because of favoritism, which didn't accurately apply either. When giving advice to new supervisors about the presence of past evals, simply ask them to use their good judgment about what they are seeing currently and weigh that against the validity of what they have read about the employee in the past.

Should a boss ever evaluate an employee on a PE anchor, job duty, or task that she or he did not ever see the employee do? This is not only an ethical issue but a legal one as well. I have seen Public Works supervisors note on an employee's eval that this person, "Operates all machinery and effectively, while using all necessary safety equipment," when the employee either has no idea and has never used certain pieces of equipment or does so unsafely. If one of your supervisors must evaluate if the employee drives a car safely as part of her or his job, then that supervisor had best get into the passenger seat while the employee takes the wheel, to see if that is so.

Here are some common PE problems that HR must help all library leaders avoid. This may involve some coaching on your part, running a quick all-leadership staff meeting on the issue, and providing sample, sanitized past evals that you would like them to model (not copy).

The Halo Effect. Here, the boss sees the employee as quasi-angelic, able to do no wrong. The eval is not accurate because the employee can and should improve on certain work performance or behavioral issues.

Overly Lenient/Overly Harsh. Favoritism or bias can come into play here, where the supervisor overlooks issues that need to be addressed for one employee and hammers another one, who may not even be as bad as described. HR needs to pay careful attention to these concerns, to avoid true claims of racism, sexism, and other biases.

Vanilla Scores/Middle Grades/Grade Inflation. Everybody gets the same scores and the same language on their evals, usually a middle of the road or what we called in college a "Gentleman's C." This makes the PE process ineffective, especially when employees share their scores, as they are likely to do, and see that everyone got the same. This creates trust problems in both the PE process and the supervisor who does this.

The Recency Error. This is the "What have you done for me lately?" problem and it manifests in positive and negative ways. "You helped three little kids learn to read last week, so that should cover the value of your contribution to the entire library and your PE will be completed accordingly!" Or, "You parked in my 'Bosses Only' parking space seven months ago and I have never forgiven you for it." We must tell all bosses to consider the employee over the entire rating period, good and what needs improvement. (This speaks to why all leaders need to keep coaching files on each of their employees, as I discussed in chapter 5, so as not to have to have the memory of an elephant.)

The Buddy System. "This employee is an old friend, we came up through the organization together, and since I'm now his or her supervisor, I will take care of him or her on the eval." This is not fair to the other employees and it can lead to a sense of entitlement among some employees, who always expect higher scores than their peers from "my pal, the boss," even when their work effort doesn't support them.

Too Many Categories. An HR director from a large library once told me, "We have a five-point scale to rate our employees, but no one ever gets a five. If I get an eval with an employee that shows a five, I send it back to the manager or supervisor with a note to change it." "Why can't someone ever get a five?" I asked. "Because," said the HRD, "no is ever that perfect. Our employees can get a 4.2 or even a 4.6, but never a five." When I asked what the difference was between a 4.2 employee and a 4.6 employee, the conversation ended abruptly. You can guess that the bosses and the employees despised the PE process because (five-point) success was forbidden.

The use of too many anchors—which can be defined as tasks or functions the employee has or has not met—is confusing to the rater and ratee alike. Simpler is always better. I have never liked using decimal points—hence the stupid conversation about 4.2 and 4.6 employees above—because it makes no sense and it's counterproductive to use the PE as a coaching tool if no one can understand those shades of gray differences. Use a five-point rating scale if you must, but no decimal points.

A One-Size-Fits-All Form. I scratch my head when I see organizations try to use one form to help rate every employee, at every level. You need to have at least two versions of your PE form: a leadership version and an employee version. The library director will use the leadership form to assess her or his department heads and/or managers; managers will use this form to rate the supervisors who work for them (with some modifications to the measurements or anchors, based on job duties at that level). And the supervisors and PICs should use the employee version to evaluate their full-time and part-time employees (they need evaluations too).

Measuring the Employee Outside the Date Range. Remind your bosses that the PE form needs to cover the employee during the rating period only. It's not a collection of the employee's many sins or clever accomplishments from seven years ago until today. If your library evaluates employees annually, then that is the only acceptable range, same as with twice a year, or my favorite, quarterly.

This brings up another issue: How do bosses rate their employees if they took over their supervision midway through the rating period or have not had a chance to see a whole year's worth of their work performance and behavior? This doesn't mean they can skip the exercise; even a few months of observation can help them draw basic conclusions. They simply use that language in their evals: "I have only seen the work and interactions of Employees A, B, and C for the past three months. As such, my general conclusions are . . ."

Fuzzy Language. "Be better, get with the program, jump on board" are all examples of imprecise, useless terminology in PEs. Worse yet, if English is not the employee's first language, she or he may have no understanding of what certain Western colloquialisms even mean: "get on the ball," "step up to the plate," and so on. Tell supervisors to broom this language out and replace it with details, examples, job functions the employee can actually do, and goals she or he can meet. We need to use performance improvement-based language and not label-based.

Punishment Phrases. Supervisors need to completely avoid using broad-based, non-specific threats of discipline or threats made to the employee in the PE. "You had better get with the program . . . or else!" not only means nothing, but these types of scare tactics can get you on the road to a lawsuit. Just like we should never use the "Bright Future" language with employees, as in, "Oh no! We will never fire you! You have a bright future here and are far too valuable to ever get rid of." These kinds of promises of "forever employment" or "one more mistake and you're out!" can cause us a lot of grief later when we do need to terminate the employee or they claim that we are targeting or retaliating against them. We use PIPs and BIPs to foreshadow discipline.

Biases. Here, the employee on the receiving end of a negative PE may claim that her or his boss was being unfair, based on being biased toward the person's race, gender, sexual orientation, or any number of protected class factors. The employee may claim the supervisor was discriminatory, retaliatory for some past issue, overly judgmental, or was too harsh on her or him and too lenient on others.

Not Done or Not Done Regularly. Variations of this include not meeting with the employee. Saying, "Just sign this and put it in my In-Box" is rude to the employee and fails to use the PE as the gateway to a formal coaching meeting. Skipping years—which sends the message to the employees that the whole process, when done sporadically, is not really that important. No enforcement of the PIPs and BIPs often happens because of this last concern.

Bosses with No Courage to See, Write, and Speak the Truth. The PE process is a critical part of being a boss. It helps with future coaching discussions, it tells the employees where they stand with us, and it urges accountability and responsibility upon our employees. It's not just a friendly chat; it's a coaching and employee development conversation that should have both merit and weight. It requires a commitment by the bosses to not only do the necessary review of each employee's efforts, accomplishments, and potential shortcomings, but also to put those words on paper, warts and all, and have the necessary conversation about the PE document and the plan for the coming rating period. As such, this requires management courage.

THREE PE SUPPORT TOOLS FOR RELUCTANT MANAGERS AND SUPERVISORS

If you don't work at or run the perfect HR world, it's possible you may have managers and supervisors who feel stressed by the PE process and as such, don't do their best work. This creates a disservice to their employees and the supportive, nourishing, but always measuring culture you are trying to create for them and the organization. Consider helping make their path to better PE documents with these three tools:

1. Go online to Amazon, the www.SHRM.org site, or your favorite HR-related bookseller, and buy every manager and supervisor in your library a *PE PHRASE BOOK*. There are many out there and you may have a preferred favorite. I have used one that has been in print since 1978 and has sold over 1.5 million copies in updated versions, from James E. Neal Jr., called *Effective Phrases for Performance Appraisals*. Armed with a current phrase book and sanitized PE versions provided by you that they can use as templates, they can feel more confident in their creation of each document for each employee. (Remind your bosses when you give them these books not to write like a robot, e.g., "Insert [employee name] here") They should not be using

cookie-cutter phrases, where every PE is either copied straight from their books or written with the exact same language for each one.

The PE phrase book has an obvious two-way value for PE authors because what is described as a positive is just as well described as a negative. "The employee uses all required personal protective equipment when using warehouse machinery" or "The employee fails to use all required personal protective equipment when using warehouse machinery."

2. Have your leaders encourage their employees to keep a "Me File." The employee-generated "Me File" is a collection of her or his accomplishments during the rating period. These are all good things, and the reason we ask the employees to keep track of what they have done is that the managers or supervisors may not have seen, recalled, or gathered themselves. The presence of the "Me File" makes it easier for the manager or supervisor to create a PE that celebrates what the employee has done, including:

- Emails, commendations, memos, and letters from patrons, co-workers, managers, or supervisors, offering kudos for good service or for contributing to a team project.
- Training classes they have attended.
- Classes taken toward degrees, and certifications.
- Projects completed successfully.
- Professional development activities.
- Library-related community activities, or charity work on behalf of the library.

Some employees complain that their co-workers get higher PE scores or an Above Standard, rating, even though "we both did the same amount of work." To put it in a brutually honest and simple way, "They had a full Me File and you offered nothing. Their efforts to keep track of their accomplishments made it easier for me to justify their Above Standard rating."

3. Have your bosses keep a Coaching File on each of their subordinates. As I discussed in more detail in chapter 5 on the value of coaching, the purpose of keeping a coaching file for each employee is to help bosses remember the details of coaching conversations, projects assigned, goals met or not, continuing performance or behavioral issues, compliance with policies, and so forth. As you'll recall, it is *not* a secondary personnel file. It doesn't contain any information about discipline, worker's compensation, medical leave. It's not a file used to ambush the employee; she or he can look at it at any time, to better understand how her or his boss will craft an accurate personnel file and the accompanying performance evaluation documents.

PE MEETING STEPS

Here's how to run a smooth, successful, and drama-free Performance Evaluation meeting (at least in my perfect HR world). Be ready to address the employee possibly using distractions from the main conversation, like excuses, minimizations, denials, rationalizations, and blaming. Stick to your themes, acknowledge you have heard what they have said, and consider the validity. Then get your focus back on to solutions or necessary changes.

1. Plan for the meeting; review the employee's PE form, along with her or his coaching file.
2. Open the meeting with a review of the themes to be covered.
3. Define the measurements on the PE form.
4. Start with an overview, then move to specifics.
5. Discuss the business impact of any problem areas.
6. Describe the employee's strengths.
7. Discuss the need for performance improvement, behavior improvement, and/or a career development plan.
8. Close the meeting with thanks, and a recap of what you both discussed (whether they agreed with all of it or not). Make certain they have a copy of their PE before they leave.

THE ROAD TO LITIGATION

As our lawyer friends have told us since the dawn of the printing of the Gutenberg Bible, "If it didn't get written down, it didn't happen." (I have stood gazing up at his statue in Strasbourg, France; very cool.) The value of the PE document is that it spells out what has happened, what needs to be done, and serves as a reminder if those changes are being made. Where organizations get sued, they have usually failed to use PEs, and have tried to get struggling employees to change based on using countless verbal (accusatory) conversations (not memorialized in follow-up emails and certainly not recalled by the employees at a later date in court). Not using PEs and not using documented coaching meetings sets up the following list of stepping-stones to the courthouse:

- No meeting about the PE document (often because it wasn't ever done or done regularly) and the subsequent expectations about work performance and/or work behavior.
- Miscommunications about expectations.

- Misinterpretations about how to change and what to do differently.
- Mismanagement; inconsistent daily supervision; poor overall leadership.
- No clear record of issues (dates, times, examples of policy violations, poor quality work, or missed deadlines, etc.).
- Employee is not clear on the performance or behavior issues to be changed and the escalating or progressive consequences for failing to make those changes.
- Management has not provided training in areas where the employee is deficient.
- Clear evidence of bias, harassment, discrimination, and/or retaliation.
- The PE is used as punishment, only focusing on the negatives, or the employee's "year-long collection of sins."

One NEAT corrective-step remedy to many of these—along with HR oversight and HR interventions to prove them in the first place—is provided by my labor law colleague, David Monks, Esq., from the Fuller Law Group in San Diego:[1]

Notice of the problem.
Explanation of how to improve.
Assistance to improve.
Time to improve.

Documenting your NEAT steps—and training your managers and supervisors to do likewise—offers a solid remedy to the list of courthouse concerns listed above.

EMPLOYEE REACTIONS TO PERFORMANCE EVALUATIONS

Dealing with the range of employee reactions to formal HR meetings takes patience, stamina, empathy, and a firm tone. No employee should be able to intimidate you or any manager or supervisor into changing your collective mind. Let's consider the range of emotions you in HR and/or your department directors, managers, or supervisors may encounter when having meetings with certain employees about coaching, verbal warnings, written warnings, changes in job duties, delegated tasks, performance evaluations, and other directed tasks that often have "Bad News" written on them. You may have to deal with some of these reactions and you may have to train your leaders to deal with them. (After all, you cannot and should not be expected to sit in on every single PE meeting with their people.) What do we do if the employee:

Sits like a statue, provides no reactions, and makes no comments? This could be a personality flaw, a long-standing feud with the supervisor, where the employee once felt disrespected and never forgot it. The employee could be a solid introvert and is too nervous to contribute. The remedy is to get through the meeting, fully explaining the PE document, and asking if the employee has questions. If not, wrap up the meeting.

Cries? My record for making both male and female employees cry during difficult, emotional, high-stress coaching meetings is quite high. This doesn't surprise me or deter me, since in almost every case, they were near tears when they walked in the room and what I said was not the trigger for that reaction. Albrecht's Law of Tears is "no snot, then the tears aren't real." Why would I be so cruel? Because some people will cry to get us to end tough HR-related meetings. I give the person a short break, ask them to come back in once she or he is ready to continue, and then I finish the discussion. Tears should not stop the conversation, otherwise that will become the employee's method to disrupt a hard talk.

Argues each point? This is common with strident employees, both during the PE meeting, coaching meetings, and often during discipline meetings. Remedy: "Let me talk all the way through this document, without interrupting, and then I'll turn it over to you for your response, okay?"

Is insubordinate? This shows up with eye-rolling, arms crossed, scowling, sighing, and breaking eye contact in a dismissive way. Similar to meeting with the statue, there may be an ulterior or interior motive that gives the employee her or his own "permission" to act this way. Stay on the form, don't shorten the meeting because you feel intimidated, and stick to your themes.

Threatens to sue? This is the approach the library champion often takes. Don't argue about the validity of this person's litigation chances. Don't make inflammatory statements like, "This is all your fault!" or "We'll see you in court!" Stick to the PE and get through it as a professional. Lots of people who threaten to sue their employer don't actually do it once they find it's not as easy as filing some papers. A variation on this response is the employee who threatens to "bring in the union rep or my association rep." They have this right if it's a true Weingarten Meeting, but PE meetings are not those (and should not be) because we don't use them to initiate discipline at that exact moment. Any pending discipline should be formally noticed in a subsequent meeting.

Is overly (and falsely) agreeable? I'm suspicious of employees who wholeheartedly agree with everything during coaching, PE, or discipline meetings. It feels insincere because it's my experience that they do this not because they think we're right as either HR or as bosses, but to simply end the meeting as soon as possible. When I have had those kinds of rushed discussions, I end them by saying, "I appreciate your enthusiastic replies and desires to change or comply. I also want you to know I hope you aren't just telling me what I want to hear and that I expect to see those changes get made."

SOME FINE POINTS

Do our rising stars/shining stars need a performance evaluation? Improvement? After all, they're doing great! What could they possibly improve? Everyone is entitled to feedback and if it's almost entirely positive so much the better. With our best performers, perhaps the PE discussion can shift to their career goals, promotional plans, and how you can help them move into more supervisory or leadership roles, for example, being the PIC for a shift, running a team for a week when their boss is on vacation, attending public meetings on behalf of the library or the director.

How do we prove success after the PE meetings? Where do we look for observable changes in employees, especially when they have a long hill to climb to get back to even average/acceptable performance? Look for improvements in interactions with patrons and co-workers, more respectful behavior during staff meetings, a more positive attitude, more responsible behavior, on-time attendance that lasts, and more accountability about their contribution to the organization.

NOTE

1. Albrecht, S., personal communication, September 17, 2020.

Chapter 8

Keeping Things Legal

Working with Your Attorneys

SPECIFIC GUIDANCE WITH THE HR ALPHABET

Some of my HR colleagues are absolute wizards when it comes to understanding and legally and accurately implementing the Family Medical Leave Act (FMLA), the Americans with Disabilities Act (ADA), and the Fair Credit Reporting Act (FCRA), which is the set of laws that covers the release of information during applicant background checks. They are comfortable with the definitions and case laws surrounding the concepts of Equal Employment Opportunity (EEO) and the city, county, state, and federal offices therein that coordinate the various activities that prevent discrimination, retaliation, and unfair hiring and supervising practices. They know the language of their most recent union contract, for example, Memo of Understanding (MOU), often because they helped negotiate many of the stipulations, rules, and agreements. They are comfortable with these laws and guidelines, perhaps because they are just way smarter than me, or they learned all the nuances from both time in grade and on-the-job experience. It's also possible they learned from making mistakes with these complexities and had to be educated by their labor law attorney.

Some of the best reports I have ever read—HR, accident, incident, after-action—were written by people who had to learn the hard way, by getting sued, deposed, schooled, or embarrassed. These are tough ways to gain their knowledge, but they certainly were better on the other side of all that.

I have found that the second-best way to educate yourself as to these various portions of our HR world is to spend a lot of time with your attorney, getting brought up to speed. This can be expensive, time-consuming, laborious, and like drinking from the word salad firehose. If you have the time, money, and inclination, and your labor law attorney has the skills and desire to educate you, then set up enough one-on-one sessions so you feel comfortable going forward on these issues alone.

The best way to fill in the gaps in your HR important legal issues knowledge is to take every opportunity to continue your education, weekly, monthly, or at least quarterly for sure, by signing up for every webinar, training luncheon, and continuous education program you can find in the areas where you feel deficient. These can be found at your local Society for Human Resources Management (SHRM) chapter (you may have to drive a bit to attend a lunch-and-learn) or through their online programs. More often, I see cutting-edge programs offered by law firms, live and online, for no fee or a small registration charge. These can range in length from a brown bag lunch session at a local hotel conference center or a restaurant with a meeting room, to a full-day "boot camp," where you get a full run-through on the most recent updates on these subjects.

Consider the HR issues that were not even on our radar screens ten years ago: work-from-home policies; a "no vaping in the workplace" policy; preventing discrimination based on hairstyles or intentionally misrepresenting someone's gender; using personal pronouns in workplace correspondence; and a favorite from the pandemic years—vaccine and mask mandates.

It can be hard to keep up with everything and still get your work done. Get the proper, qualified help.

USING LEGAL SERVICES

If I have one pet peeve about articles in most HR magazines (and I would say I see it most often in SHRM's *HR Magazine*), it would be how many times I see an otherwise informative article, either written by a freelancer, an HR practitioner, or someone who works in HR, and the concluding paragraph is always some version of the same: "Consult with your labor law attorney for more guidance."

This is the same language you see in nearly every academic paper and journal article, where the conclusion is some form of the phrase, "The conclusion of this far-reaching and years-long study of the data is that more study of the data is needed."

In other words, work begets more work. I get the advice to reach out to your attorney, but that seems to be the default concluding paragraph, just like the car dealer says "Your Mileage May Vary" when it comes to fuel efficiency for the car you just bought. Use your good judgment, meaning if you think the issue needs legal scrutiny, because it's outside what you normally do, it's an entirely new set of federal or state laws that will determine your approach, or has the real potential for future litigation (see my rant below on how easy it is to sue someone and how hard it is to successfully sue some-one), then get advice. If those criteria are not in place, use your wisdom, experience, and common sense, without having to pay for the advice you already know. I have seen too many skilled HR directors and managers doubt their judgment and thereafter create an attachment to their legal services providers which wasn't necessary.

If you have access to a skilled labor law attorney, that person is a valuable ally. Let's talk about how you can get the best legal advice, recognizing the advantages, limits, and motivations of our attorney friends.

If you were working in the HR department for a large or global firm, you would have access to a legal department, which could answer your questions via an email or a phone call. Chances are good the lawyers there would be paid a better-than-decent salary to respond to your queries for advice. If you worked HR at a smaller firm, chances are good they would have a one-person legal department—an attorney on-site who is generalist, with knowledge in many areas: contracts, risk management, labor law, insurance, worker's compensation, and so forth.

Most other examples of legal services would come from an offsite law office, where you would receive a certain number of legal advice hours covered under a monthly retainer, or in other cases, on a billable hourly basis. This is quite common with my city/county library clients, where they receive legal advice from the city attorney, county attorney, town counsel, or other similarly named law office, who is either elected to that position by the voters or, more likely, chosen by the elected officials for your city or town. (Your city council, county board of supervisors, town council, board of alderman, etc.)

In the small cities I work for in California, the designated "City Attorney" who is selected to handle all legal questions for that entity is often doing the same for several other nearby small cities. If you have the same setup for your city, this often means the lawyer in question is juggling your information request with many other city departments or even other cities completely. You may hear more from this person's paralegal or legal assistant than from him or her.

BEST USES OF YOUR ATTORNEY'S WISDOM

One of my challenges as an HR consultant was to help new or newly revamped HR departments develop policies. I would often come in and be asked to rewrite policies that hadn't been updated since the 1990s, or to create new policy language for legal issues that just came down from the EEOC,

OSHA, or the Department of Labor, at either or both the federal and state levels.

If you have been asked to write policies from scratch, staring at a blank screen and waiting for inspiration is not fun. I quickly found that using templates or existing policy language (best borrowed from similar agencies) was my best and fastest path to success. 'Tis far better to start from 100 words and get to 1,000 than to start at zero and try to reach 1,000, struggling along the way.

Our HR lawyer friends appreciate the same approach: they would rather work with what you give them than have to draft it themselves. They certainly can, having access to plenty of templates and boilerplate policies, but it's just easier for them (and cheaper for you) if you can give them the most complete draft language you can. You want to ask them to improve upon it, protect your agency, add value, and make it readable.

Here are some examples where you may need their help. (Note that these are ranked in a bit of a cradle-to-grave order, to follow the employee's path from applicant to retirement, or probation failure to subsequent termination, depending on how things go.)

- Review of job application forms, job testing protocols, job duties, and job descriptions.
- Interview questions.
- On-boarding and orientation forms and new-hire processes and procedures.
- Probationary period protocols.
- Performance evaluation forms.
- Performance Improvement Plans (PIPs) and Behavior Improvement Plans (BIPs).
- Discipline policies and practices.
- Termination policies and practices.
- Compliance with FMLA and ADA reasonable accommodation requests.
- Workers' compensation policies and practices.
- Exit interview questions.
- Benefits, retirement, and severance packages.

Other useful projects that can benefit from their review and advice:

- Review of your salary surveys, compensation studies, and advice on keeping pay rates fair and legal.
- New federal and state government legislation connected to the HR function.
- General HR policy development and review.
- Help with your ongoing HR audits and operational reviews.

- Help with deciding when to delete e-records and shred hard-copy files within a timeframe that is legal and reasonable. (Just like you're supposed to keep your personal tax records for seven years, there is a limit to everything and electronic and physical file storage is not supposed to be infinite. Some states say one year, others four, others six, and a few say seven years. Ask what your state requires and what your legal advisors prefer, which may be different spans.)

GETTING THE BEST FROM YOUR LEGAL ADVISORS

A few items of note to help with your interaction with the legal eagles at your side:

Billable chats. Your email or phone call starts the clock ticking. Many law firms ask their attorneys to bill in fifteen-minute intervals, all day long. Most firms ask their attorneys (especially the new associates) to bill at least 1,500 hours per calendar year, somewhere, somehow, to their collection of clients. Considering there are supposedly 2,080 hours in a working year, that's a bunch of dollar signs. Even a short and simple question that gets a short and simple answer can generate an invoice for you. This shouldn't deter you from using legal services; it should remind you to be quick and clear in getting your needs met. Some law offices bill in six-minute increments, so even a "Hi-What About This?-Thanks-Bye" phone conversation or email costs your library money. This is not to say you need to speak at a rapid-fire pace on the phone, but save the long-winded social pleasantries for when they are officially off the clock.

Be concise in your requests. HR law is complex and changes by the day. You need to keep your information requests as specific as possible. Try not to send them off on deep-sea fishing expeditions; their time is your money.

Ask them to "add value." As to any HR or library policies you send over for their review, tell them to add value, not just more pages. This is a coded phrase they should correctly interpret as, "Don't add more words to what I have sent you for the sake of adding legal-sounding words." In other words, your legal advisor may think he or she has to account for every potentially catastrophic possibility (Just Google "force majeure, "acts of God," "weather-related events," and "strikes and labor disputes," for the ultimate example of what could go wrong, but probably won't).

Ask them to write in plain English. One of my favorite attorney jokes is, "I love lawyers. They're the only people in the world who can write a 20,000-word document and call it a 'brief.'"

Whatever they do for you, it should be able to be read, interpreted accurately, and fully understood when read by a non-lawyer. No one wants to read HR policies that say, "Party of the first part, hereafter identified as 'Employee,' will provide labor services for the party of the second part, hereafter known as 'Employer' . . ."

Recall your last big purchase: your car, your house, your condo, even an apartment rental leasing contract, or a piece of software, with the six-page on-screen "EULA" (end user license agreement). Did you read every word of those documents? Few of us ever do. Give me the pen and then the keys is our usual approach or just keep clicking until the software starts to function.

Some younger attorneys were taught in law school that plain English agreements, policies, and contracts are (big shock) just as enforceable and legally valid as the old-school word salads. My discussion with HR attorneys is this, "The more clear you can make the document, the easier it is for the reader, applicant, employee, other department, or insurance company to understand it. Less confusion means fewer questions, and fewer delays in deciding, signing, or acting on the document, right?" Some of them will agree completely and still send over an overly long screed that is repetitive, confusing, and therefore often forces the other side to bring in another lawyer to interpret it.

Stick to your guns on this issue. Longer is not necessarily better. Ask for the documents your HR lawyer returns to you to be clear and concise.

LET'S TALK ABOUT YOUR ROLE IN HR-RELATED LITIGATION

I have mixed feelings when I hear HR people say, "We could get sued!" either by a current employee, a soon-to-be ex-employee, or a recently terminated employee. This cry of anguish is in part true and unlikely, unless our behavior as an organization has been egregious, repetitive, and obviously discriminatory or retaliatory. These last phrases are often used by plaintiffs' lawyers, in their civil suit filings, to try and convince the judge that their case has merit. Just because a lawyer says our conduct was "unconscionable, outrageous, and shocking" doesn't make it so; that's for the judge to decide and these things require proof, not just angry claims.

Fear of being sued leads some HR professionals to keep employees who should be fired for poor performance and toxic behavior, to the detriment of the team, department, and organization. I have seen many examples where the employee who is on thin ice talks to his or her spouse/partner/friend "who works in HR or the legal field" and comes to the office one day, spouting phrases like "hostile work environment," "whistleblower," and "damages for my pain and suffering." Sometimes these blowhard phrases have the wrong

impact, which is to convince seemingly intelligent and correct HR professionals that their judgment to ask for a course correction in the employee's
behavior or performance is somehow wrong and should be withdrawn for
consideration.

I've spoken with plenty of my labor law pals about this strategy some
employees use—"Leave me alone or I'll sue you!"—and they have given me
a reality check which may help calm our collective fears. Yes, organizations
can get sued, but I would argue not always easily and not always successfully.
Anyone can take a car, bus, Uber, or spaceship to the local courthouse and
file a lawsuit against anyone they choose. These people are often called *pro
per* or *pro se* plaintiffs, because they represent themselves. The most useful
identifying reasons that we can see that they represent themselves is because:
they have spoken to one or more (or a dozen) lawyers, who have all turned
them down; they are furiously angry and want to retaliate against their former
organizations and their bosses; and finally, they want to cause you to spend
time, money, and hassle getting their flimsy cases dismissed.

There is a presumption among some wounded current or former employees that the woods are full of hungry attorneys just waiting to take on a case
against Big Library (or Big City or Big County) to teach them a lesson and
to "make certain this type of harm never comes to another employee." These
"clients" believe these same attorneys will take on a case on a contingency
basis, without requiring a retainer and advancing all the expenses (filing fees,
copying requests, depositions of experts, etc.) all in the pursuit of justice.
Perhaps they have acquired this "No Money Down" perception from seeing the countless billboards, radio, TV, and Internet ads from auto accident
attorneys who tell them they will take their case for nothing and "We Only
Get Paid When We Win." Back in the real world where we work, even if a
labor law attorney will take a case (often after a lengthy phone or in-office
screening process done by their paralegals or themselves), it will require the
aggrieved plaintiff to put up his or her own money to start the process. This
often puts the brakes on even the most vehement plaintiff. Just because you
get sued doesn't mean you necessarily did anything wrong, at any point in
the employment cycle process. Some people just like to file lawsuits; some
of those people get an attorney to agree they have a case and some won't, but
that rarely stops them from trying.

Lawyers are usually quite good at vetting cases early enough to see if they
can win it or not. Unless there is a chance to become part of a class action suit,
or the defendant has deep pockets (Walmart for both, to use two examples of
expensive litigation that the store chain lost, or at least settled for millions),
or the plaintiff current or former employee is a senior executive (making millions) suing a company he or she formerly ran (for millions), most lawyers
are not interested. (You might add in the lawyer who believes he or she has

a chance to generate a lot of media coverage and free publicity, and so will take on the case at his or her own cost.)

One of my legal colleagues tells me her usual response to a current or former employee who threatens litigation is this, "Fine. Have your lawyer get in touch with me and I'll either handle the case myself or refer it to our insurance provider, who will assign one of their staff attorneys to it." What she would like to add is, "Our army of civil litigation attorneys—who only do labor law defense and specialize in working on behalf of organizations—will outlast, outwit, and outplay your lawyer, who may handle your case, after you give him or her a $5,000 retainer, as a starter fee."

This is not to say I take being sued lightly. It can be expensive and time-consuming to quash frivolous lawsuits and expensive, time-consuming, and emotional to defend yourself and your department's actions in a suit that has some merit. Judges and juries don't always see things our way.

More commonly, your library may be represented by an insurance company and its attorneys will recommend a settlement—"in the interest of swift justice"—even though they agree your agency did nothing wrong. While this may cause outrage in you—"Why don't we fight if we know we're right?"—it's more about spending money now to save money later for your lawyers. Best to give the plaintiff $10,000 in go-away money now than to risk having a judge or jury award him or her $100,000 two years from now.

I have heard far too many stories of plaintiff employees who were, in point of fact, paid off by insurance company attorneys who either did not want to go to court (and some lawyers are courtroom-aversive, since it takes them out of their comfort zone) or thought that they were making the best business decision.

You may argue accurately, but ultimately unsuccessfully, against settling a wrongful termination or a harassment case, because your office did nothing wrong, procedurally or administratively. The best you can do is to make your case, provide proof of your organization's due diligence, and let the lawyers and their insurers decide, without taking it personally.

Keep All of Your Documents Orderly and Accessible

Even seemingly random emails can make a big difference, to prove that you, your managers, or your employees did or did not do what is being alleged. In litigation issues, your office may be served with a "subpoena duces tecum," which is a legal demand for all documents pertaining to a particular issue. That seemingly ominous request in an employment case may ask for all documents in a terminated employee's employment file—his or her original application and onboarding package; performance evaluations; notes from coaching discussions; Performance or Behavior Improvement Plans; discipline events; and so on.

I have seen subpoenas ask for every email where an employee was mentioned, from the date of hire to the termination date. Some of these ask for more than can be successfully gathered and provided, and they know that, but they still ask for the moon and the stars and box to carry them in. Your attorney can often successfully quash some of the more outrageous demands by telling the other side that the documents don't exist because they were legally and rightfully disposed of years ago.

Keep Strict Confidentiality

Treat each business-related conversation with every employee as if it were confidential, even when it seems sort of casual. When it comes to litigation issues, this is more than important. Do not share any information with current or former employees, elected or appointed officials, other department heads, or certainly, the media, which might pertain to the case at hand. You can certainly discuss the litigation process with your bosses, the named parties (using good judgment as to how much you share), and with your attorneys. But never forget how small the world really is and using the "Six Degrees of Kevin Bacon" rule that sooner or later everyone knows everyone, what you say, even in passing or as a joke, can come up later in court or hurt your defense.

It's amazing how the employee who can't remember what you told him or her yesterday can remember what you said about another employee two years ago. We ask employees not to discuss their salaries with each other (even though these are often posted online as part of them being city, county, or state employees), in order to keep the backbiting to a minimum. And yet they still do. I recall doing a series of coaching conversations with an employee who was furious because his co-worker made six cents more per hour than he did, to do the same job. This was due to a clerical error that was never caught, five or six years after they were both hired. The aggrieved employee would not let that go and to get him back to work, I had the Payroll Department calculate the difference and send him a check.

We ask employees not to discuss their individual performance evaluation meetings with each other or not to share their PE documents, and they do. This often causes resentments, jealousies, and howls of bias, favoritism, or targeting, even when the PEs are spot-on accurate, legal, and fair.

And we ask employees not to discuss their statements in any sexual or racial harassment or misconduct investigations, but of course, they overshare with each other about those discussions too.

You cannot always control what they say to each other, even if your policies forbid these conversations during HR investigations, but you can model what you expect from the employees by not oversharing yourself.

Research the Legal Process Steps in Your State

You may know these steps from having been involved in previous litigation events and they certainly vary from state to state, but it's important to be familiar with the typical process for an HR-related civil suit. It can start as such:

Notice of Service and the Initial Complaint. Where your library and its leaders, your city/county and its leaders, and even you are named in a civil suit.

Request for discovery of documents. Where the other side's lawyer(s) ask for relevant documents. Your attorney(s) will typically decide if these requests are "overbroad," outside the scope of the litigation elements, or undeliverable because they are not retrievable, either in electronic or physical form.

Interrogatories. These are often specific questions asked about the received discovery documents. This process can go back and forth for quite a bit.

Various response requests and motions. Usually, these are done to amend the initial complaint; add more defendants or torts to the initial filing; change the court of venue (move it up from a superior court to state court or to federal court); or request that a judge support or quash certain process steps as the litigation goes forward.

MSJ request to a judge. This is a Motion for Summary Judgment, where the motion asks the court to decide on at least one claim in the litigation that the other side feels can be excluded. The decision on this motion can stop the entire litigation process or simply remove one element and continue on with the remaining concerns to be decided in court.

Depositions of primary parties, related witnesses, and/or both sides' experts and their reports. If you have ever been deposed, you know it is a stressful experience. A lot of people wearing suits are staring at you and asking you tough questions, for an event or an employee that worked for your library three years ago. Most depositions these days are videotaped, which is made easier when they are done via an electronic meeting medium, like Zoom. Your attorney(s) or the other side may depose various current or former employees, bosses, or leaders. Each side may depose the others' HR experts and go over every line of their respective reports carefully. (I have been deposed about a dozen times and each one has been an exercise in my patience and preparation.)

Pre-trial settlement meetings. If you consider that the national average for civil trials that actually end up in court in front of a jury ranges from state to state from about 4 to 10 percent, there is a good chance your case will end before the trial portion begins. Judges prefer this approach, to speed things along and keep their courtrooms open for complex cases or for those that have little hope of settling. There is no way of knowing what will settle and what will go to court, as the dollar amounts, at least in the thirty-plus cases I've been on as an expert witness, seem to make no difference that I can see. I have been on the defense side of cases where the demand was for 100 million dollars and it settled three days before the trial. I have been on small-dollar plaintiff cases which went all the way to a jury trial.

Trial, in front of a judge alone or a jury. Like the deposition process, you may be called on to testify on behalf of your library and its or your HR practices, in front of a judge or a jury. The rules are the same as for a deposition: ask what is answered, don't embellish beyond that; tell the truth, even if you think it hurts your case, because there is nothing worth lying for; and go home knowing that you did your best, honestly and professionally.

Appeal process. Guess what? Depending on the outcome, you may get to do the entire thing all over again! I was on the plaintiffs' side of a sexual harassment case that took four years to get to trial and then started again with an appeal right after it was over. I was on the plaintiffs' side of a wrongful death/no background check case where the defendant company hired a maintenance employee who murdered a woman in the apartment building where he worked. My side won the case, the judge disagreed with the dollar amount the jury gave the woman's family, and we started all over again. That took six years.

Be prepared to devote several years of your life to this event. Unlike TV and movie courtroom dramas, justice is not swift.

Chapter 9

Harassment Investigations

Awareness, Response, Conclusions, and Consequences

My experience with this issue in my library security consulting work is admittedly one-sided. While I have heard of incidents of library staff sexually or racially harassing each other, it's exceedingly rare for me to have worked on this issue with library employees as the cause. It's not the library employees and we already know who causes this problem, almost entirely.

Unfortunately, based on what I have been told by library leaders, HR professionals, and library staffers, the biggest culprits and the highest number of incidents of sexual or racial harassment are caused by male library patrons.

According to data from the American Library Association (ALA), the percentage of female employees to males, across all levels in a typical city/county library is about 70–30.[1] Your library may be represented differently but like nursing, K–6 teaching, and real estate, women dominate the population of these professions over men. That's not to say that women don't ever engage in any forms of harassment against each other or male employees, or that male employees in libraries have never engaged in the harassment of others, just that I have more experience handling this issue in traditionally male-based professions involving fire, police, construction, maintenance, and Public Works employees.

Even though the passage of Title VII of the 1964 Civil Rights Act made sexual harassment in the workplace illegal behavior, it continues today, often in different, more insidious forms. Other newer examples discussed in the April 2024 Equal Employment Opportunity Commission (EEOC) harassment prevention guidelines include harassment that takes place during work from home meetings, as employees are interacting on Zoom or Teams platforms; employees who are not "out" with their sexuality choice but who are outed by co-workers without their consent; same-sex harassment; racial harassment based on different skin tones or hairstyles; or the harassment or misgendering of transgender employees.

Sexual or racial harassment prevention will always require management vigilance, multiple channels of reporting, an investigative process, updated policies that support victims and punish perpetrators, and the necessary courage for all employees to report if they are harassed or witness other employees being harassed. We need to tell employees: "Just because it's not happening directly to you doesn't make it acceptable behavior. If you were a bystander or a witness to sexually or racially harassing behaviors, you need to have the courage to tell our directors, managers, supervisors (the ones not involved in these behaviors), HR, or the library attorney what you have seen, overheard, or were told by other targeted employees, who may be too afraid of retaliation to report it themselves. We must address unprofessional conduct that violates our policies and we can't fix what we don't know about."

All employees have the right to a work environment that does not allow sexual or racial harassment from anyone, including directors, managers, supervisors, co-workers, colleagues, or vendors, visitors, or customers. Our employees need to tell our personnel stakeholders if these behaviors are happening to them or around them so HR can address, investigate, and stop them, as soon as possible.

Similar scenarios are possible that don't necessarily happen inside the actual workplace. There are certain acts that by their very nature are unprofessional conduct, plainly and simply. Our message to all employees must be clear: "You have a right not to be exposed to sexual or racial harassment during work-related activities or in settings that have a reasonable connection to the workplace. This includes driving to or flying to an offsite training program with a co-worker; sitting in an offsite hotel training room, or eating meals with colleagues in restaurants as part of work-related travel. The presence of alcohol, in a hotel room or at a bar, is also not an excuse for bosses or co-workers to engage in sexually or racially harassing behaviors, even if they say they are 'just kidding' or 'joking around with everybody' these are not a defense for this illegal behavior. If you're subjected to jokes, comments, language, photos, videos, notes, or emails of a sexual or racial nature, or are physically touched in an unwanted way by anyone on a work-related business trip, you must report what happened (with as many details about dates, times, places, people, and offending conduct as possible) to our HR office."

Harassment in the work culture destroys morale, creates fear, and causes good employees to leave. It's expensive and bad for business. It's time to get back to the basics of prevention: harassment policies, annual training, constant awareness, employee reporting, and management vigilance matched with enforcement, so this disturbing issue will not continue to scar our personal and professional landscapes.

SEXUAL HARASSMENT 101

I'm going to start with a personal preference when it comes to the words I believe we need to use to describe your employees who have been racially or sexually harassed, bullied, or otherwise had their job functions interfered with. My choice is the phrase "target employee," as opposed to "victim employee." I feel the term "victim" has the wrong connotation and somehow suggests that employees are helpless in their own defense. To define it as being targeted by a harasser or a bully or another perpetrator says to me it was not their fault and it helps me to protect their rights and to enforce consequences.

The least common type of sexually oriented harassment is "Quid pro quo" (Latin for "this for that"), which is where a supervisor requests sexual favors from a job applicant or an employee, as a condition of hiring, continued employment, favorable treatment, or punishment and retaliation if refused. This type happens but is much rarer than the other—a sexually harassing work environment without a quid pro quo element. We can assume several reasons that quid pro quo is rare: it comes with severe consequences (public revelations, shaming by the media, and expensive civil suits where the harasser can be sued personally); the liability on the offending supervisor or manager's organization is "automatically attached" (as our lawyer friends like to say), meaning there is no defense for the behavior and checks must be written; and we have seen an evolution (driven in large part by the "Me Too" movement directed at famous Hollywood executives or celebrities who have sexually assaulted both women and men) where this "casting couch" behavior is no longer tolerated or ignored in our workplaces.

The most prevalent form of sexual harassment is the harassing environment: unwanted, unwelcome, repetitive, egregious, severe behavior, or a sexually harassing nature (including same-sex and transgender targets), not stopped by management, and includes members of protected classes.

I define this type as a failure of the work culture. It suggests a lack of vigilance and concern by management (even when pressed by HR professionals to make immediate changes in how these cases are investigated, corrected, and offered support for the targeted employees). There is no excuse for allowing these behaviors to flourish—and not just because they have been illegal in our workplaces since 1964—because they are wrong, unprofessional, expensive, and create an environment where employees leave or the ones who stay are miserable. We have to be better at this subject.

Let's look at the elements of a harassment-free workplace:

Policy Creation, Ongoing Development, and Making Improvements Driven by Federal and State Laws

I have testified in federal court as an expert on sexual harassment. I was working for an attorney who had two plaintiffs who were harassed multiple times by multiple males in their workplace. The primary issue I attacked in this case was the length of the defendant's harassment policy: three paragraphs. As I said at the time in a Denver federal court, "This is the shortest harassment policy I've seen in my whole career. And that is not a good thing."

There is a sense, in my experience, of a "Goldilocks and the Three Bears" about the just-right number of pages; we probably don't need thirty pages to explain the elements of the policy but three paragraphs is always going to be too short. It's not so much about the length of the policy as it is about having an adequate number of sections to address the issue fully.

Policy Education at the Leader, Manager, Supervisor, and Lead Levels

Every library leader, at every level from the director to the PIC, needs to know the details and elements of the organization's sexual and racial harassment policy. It's not enough just to have them sign a "Receipt and Acknowledgment of Policy" form and move on; they need to be able to follow the elements: paying attention, initial conversation with a targeted employee, notifying HR, supporting the investigation process by providing HR with access to evidence and witnesses, creating consequences for perpetrators, offering support for targeted employees, and showing continued vigilance for repeated events and protection from retaliation.

Policy Education at the Staff Level

Again, it's not enough for staff to simply sit through a live or online training class, sign a form that says they were given a copy of the policy, put it into their hard-copy personnel file, and move on. They need to be told what they can and cannot do, have the concept of protected classes as the necessary element of a hostile work environment claim, know about multiple channels of reporting (including being able to go outside their chain of command), cooperating and having patience through an investigation, and understanding the consequences of harassing behaviors, whether it involves a co-worker, vendor, or patron.

Training in Awareness, Prevention, and Response at the Leader, Manager, Supervisor, and PIC Level

Either taught by you in HR or using outside HR consultants with extensive knowledge in the subject, usually two hours, once per year will suffice. Document these dates, and who attended, in your training files. Review the training content each year to be sure it is current and timely. (Just having leaders go to this training is not a perfect litigation defense, but not having this training makes it harder to defend ourselves that our leaders knew or should have known what to do to prevent harassment.)

Training at the Staff Level

Usually, one hour per year will suffice; document these dates and who attended. Review the training content each year to be sure it is current and timely.

Reporting Process

This needs to include multiple channels and multiple formats; access to contact information at the US EEOC and your state's EEOC or Department of Fair Employment.

Bosses Who Are Trained to Meet with Employee-Targets

To get the details, context, and content, and prepare for a conversation and follow-up written report as to what they were told, for HR's review.

Identifying the Specific Protected Class Issue(s)

Necessary to meet the hostile work environment standard. (See my deeper dive into this important concept below.)

Evaluation of the Complaint

This includes examining the relationship and/or past history between the parties. Typically this should be done by you in your HR role.

Investigative Steps and Timeline

Interviews with the targeted employee, review of any evidence (photos, cartoons, videos, emails, texts, Security Incident Reports), interviews with witness-employees, even patrons who may have witnessed incidents, and then a conversation with the perpetrator employee or patron.

Consequences for True Perpetrators

Tell employees or patrons what they are accused of, how the behavior must stop (if it is not egregious enough to require a termination of the employee or suspension of the patron's ability to use the library), drawing new behavioral boundaries for the offender, and enforcing consequences.

Support for True Targets

Most employees don't want to come forward with these incidents because they are rightly embarrassed, humiliated, angry, and fearful. They want the behaviors to stop, but they don't want to go through the necessary investigative process to help make them stop. As an HR professional, you need to provide reassurance, empathy, and a description of the investigative process and the timeline (we don't make rash or hasty decisions when it comes to these allegations; we are thorough).

Protection from Retaliation

As a punishment aimed at targeted employees, or at employees who witnessed sexually or racially harassing behaviors, retaliation is insidious and often subtle. Whether it's done by other employees, bosses, or bosses who tell their employees to retaliate, it is not always obvious. The clear versions are harsh discipline, bullying, and firing the person without cause. The subtle types can include the silent treatment, piling on too much work or no longer assigning work, rewarding other employees and ignoring the target, allowing some employees to put in for overtime, favorable work schedules for some employees, and not providing the same information or opportunities to targeted employees.

Ongoing Vigilance

It's not enough to conclude the case and move on. This subject requires oversight of both the work culture and because we are a public-facing entity, of the patron interactions with our staff as well.

THE INVESTIGATIVE PROCESS FOR HARASSMENT AND "HOSTILE WORKPLACE" CLAIMS

In my role as an HR consultant, I have assisted dozens of HR directors and HR managers in their sexual and racial harassment investigations, working with them, or their hired licensed private investigators (as may be required in some states to do investigations—and not HR consultants—as it was when I was in California), and/or their agency's legal counsel.

If you got an instant flash of dollar signs swirling out the door when you considered consultants, PIs, or lawyers working on a harassment investigation, you are not far wrong.

ACCURATELY DEFINING THE (DREADED) "HOSTILE WORK ENVIRONMENT"

Workplace rules certainly differ from state to state, but all fifty states agree that every employee has the right to work in a workplace environment that is free from harassment, bullying, and mistreatment.

In my HR consulting and coaching experience, the problem with the hostile work environment concept is that it is widely misunderstood by most employees. Because they have either received bad advice from someone (a non-lawyer colleague or family member who took a class, once, perhaps) or misinterpreted the concept because they are angry at their employer, they believe it covers more than it does.

The concept of "protected classes" exists for employees to legally defend themselves from mistreatment in the workplace, based on being in a protected class. (My former state, California, has the most protected classes in the country, including being a domestic violence victim and having certain hairstyles.)

Violations of these laws create the concept of the "hostile workplace," which is legally defined conduct or words used by leaders or co-workers (or even vendors, contractors, or patrons) as *discriminatory, repetitive, unwelcome, severe, pervasive treatment, toward people the EEOC defines as* being in a protected class. This treatment interferes with an employee's ability to do his or her job successfully. Besides being done by bosses or co-workers, these acts, behaviors, or statements could be created by patrons, vendors, or contractors at the facility. It can also involve retaliatory actions (bullying, giving the silent treatment, not giving overtime opportunities, passing over for promotion, etc.), aimed at the targeted employee for reporting these behaviors.

Although most plaintiff lawyers would disagree with me, it upsets me when I see a reasonable, vigilant organization accused of "allowing" racial or sexual harassment—as in "they knew or should have known that it was occurring." It's one thing to have witnessed these behaviors and not done anything—out of apathy, indifference, or paralysis—and it's another to have a written policy that describes how employees can and must report harassing behaviors so they can be investigated and stopped, and yet the employee did not follow those procedures. Most harassment policies I see have some version of "multiple channels of reporting" in them (as should yours), which we need to remind our new and existing employees about. Management must be put on notice to stop these behaviors—they cannot fix what they did not know about, unless many rank-and-file employees knew about these behaviors and management chooses to avoid addressing them.

When it comes to accurately defining the "hostile work environment," I believe HR professionals should take a proactive approach and explain.

Context is critical; hurt feelings, rude people, or bad bosses do not meet the legal definition.

Wrongly considered examples prevail:

> My boss is a jerk! She's always telling me to get off the Internet and my Etsy sites, stop looking at my phone all day, and do my work!

> My co-workers have created a hostile workplace because I never get invited for coffee or out to lunch with the "chosen group."

Not a surprise, this is often because they don't like or trust this person, so they don't engage with him or her, beyond just at a basic workplace communication level. Some of them have been burned by this person, so they take the opposite approach and don't speak to him or her unless necessary.

> *Champion:* "This whole office is full of serial harassers, bullies, and co-workers who pick on me or retaliate against me when I complain about them!"

> *HR:* "That sounds serious. Can you give me some examples?"

> *Champion:* "I can't think of one right now, but you know as well as me what's happening around here!"

Despite not understanding the concept of protected classes and the true definition of a hostile work environment, they continue to see injustice everywhere and are usually furiously unsatisfied with your lack of effort to both agree with them and stop these (phantom) behaviors.

Courageous HR professionals and equally courageous managers and supervisors will say: "I'm sorry what you heard or saw seemed offensive to you. I disagree that it violates our harassment policies. I know the definitions of this state and I don't agree that you are being targeted because you are in a protected class. Not all employee interactions at work need to be regulated. I am careful, as is this entire management team, to evaluate the behavior and performance of every employee. Not everything that goes on here is aimed directly or indirectly at you. I want you to focus on your assignments and stop worrying about everyone else. Your boss has the absolute right to evaluate your work performance, using our coaching and performance evaluation processes. It's not personal; we are having a work conversation with you and will continue to do so, when needed. I will pay attention to our HR issues here; that's my role. Please go back to work."

In my view, this employee (and usually it is just one per library, we hope), is out to rescue the organization from itself, one unnecessary, unrequested complaint at a time. I refer to this person as . . .

THE LIBRARY CHAMPION

Let's continue to define their impact and approach even further.

Perhaps this library scenario is uncomfortably familiar: An employee (of either gender) is walking down the hallway when he or she hears two co-workers telling jokes across the room. These jokes aren't raunchy, but they are a little edgy.

The two co-workers aren't shouting their jokes; they're using whispered tones. The passing employee has to strain to hear the punchline, but he or she has picked up enough to be outraged. His or her next stop is your office, where the story comes out in full detail that the library workplace has become the dreaded "hostile work environment."

Not surprisingly, this employee sees similar injustices everywhere. (I once worked with a woman at the city of San Diego who kept track of the number of times people cursed in the room, not at her, but in general. Uh, news flash: this is something many employees in the workplace do, especially when tired, angry, or frustrated. If I were her boss, I would've said, "We need to give you more work to do.") The events they witness range from playful banter between two friends at work, mild nonsexual, non-physical flirting between consenting single adults on their coffee breaks, or inoffensive practical jokes.

Certain employees who see these things can become the self-appointed "champions" of employee behavior in the library. They wear out a path to the supervisor's office or worse, HR (where they may have their own name-engraved chair). They corner every manager or supervisor and rant about unfair treatment, hostile work environments, and how senior management at every level is "allowing" this to take place.

The ironic part is that while the "champion" is a great observer of the problems of others, he or she is not a very good employee. The "champion's" boss often has to walk a delicate balance when confronting his or her poor performance or nosy behavior. Any coaching session, counseling memo, or Performance Improvement Plan is met with howls of protest. Because the "champion" has blown the whistle previously, the supervisor must be retaliating against him or her. The "champion" loves to start every meeting with variations of, "Is this going into my Personnel file?" or "Do I need to call my union rep?"

ADDRESSING THE CHAMPION

Despite your desire to have your employee group act like ladies and gentlemen at work, and your need for them to get along while they do their jobs, personality conflicts can erupt. What starts as a disagreement over something small, left unaddressed, can devolve into bullying, passive-aggressive behaviors, the silent treatment, or worse, litigation, based on one employee's perception (right or wrong) of a hostile work environment.

Some employees function under the mistaken belief that every conflict between their co-workers or their supervisors is somehow a "hostile work environment." This wrongly defines the concept and can lead to a sense of entitlement, where they believe their direct supervisor, the next-level supervisor, or the HR director or HR manager must intervene and rescue them from a situation where they feel mistreated and ill-used.

When these situations first arise, it can help to have an individual meeting with the employee and say, "Look, we both know you don't have to love everybody you work with and you don't have to even *like* everybody you work with. But you must coexist and get along with the people you work with. I expect every employee in this library to be professional and respectful in their interactions with the patrons, their bosses, and their co-workers."

We should ask employees to self-manage their behavior and to solve their differences without having to "run to Mom and Dad" every time. Professional adults should work and interact professionally. So what do you do if they don't?

Because of past histories, previous problems, or when they feel the issue is unfixable, your managers, supervisors, and employees may ask HR to ride to the rescue. They may want you to intervene on their behalf and "fix" the other person, as if they weren't a stakeholder too. In these situations, where the issue is *not related to a policy violation*, like bullying, sexual or racial harassment, or harassment or discrimination related to either employee being in a protected class (age, sexual orientation, pregnancy, religion, etc.), you can suggest to both employees that you facilitate a discussion between them.

This process is not done in a parental way, where you lecture both parties about what they need to do. Rather, you explain that this is a voluntary meeting, where you will listen to both sides, help each employee set new "ground rules" about getting along, and confirm what each should expect from the other. Your function in these meetings is not to be Ruler of All You Survey or be the Be-All End-All solution-maker. Your job is to use "assisted discovery" to help them both get to a position of compromise.

So what's the solution? How do you manage entitled and poor-performing library workplace "champions"? How do you get past the distraction techniques they use to deny their ineptitude or lousy attitude? How do you talk to them about their impact on their co-workers (and bosses), without thinking you're going to get sued after every conversation?

Managing the "champion" requires *management courage*. I define this skill as both the ability and the desire to have the necessary crucial coaching conversations—about performance or behavior—with the "champion," and not be scared off by their false bravado or lawsuit threats.

The tool of choice for the courageous manager is coaching. I have defined coaching throughout this book as a non-disciplinary, performance, or behavior-changing conversation. Courageous HR professionals and the managers and supervisors they support initiate as many coaching conversations as necessary, until they don't see any changes, which is when they know it's time to switch to progressive discipline.

Dealing with the "champion" using coaching can be paradoxical. The courageous supervisor knows he or she will have to spend *more time* with the "champion," not less. "Champions" will require *more* goal-setting and more interactions with supervisors, not less, even though there is a tendency for most bosses to want to avoid them.

"Champion" employees think they win when they are given retirement packages to leave; assignments, promotions or transfers they don't deserve; or are allowed to continue to bully, browbeat, or annoy their co-workers. The courageous HR professional, manager, or supervisor who stands his or her ground can fight the "champion's" poor performance, disruptive behavior, and entitled attitude with consequences, coaching, a Performance Improvement Plan (PIP) or a Behavior Improvement Plan (BIP), and courage.

Workplace Bullying: A Tricky Concept That Needs a Policy

In 1964, when US Supreme Court Justice Potter Stewart was asked to describe his test for obscenity, he was said to have remarked, "I know it when I see it." (Another version of this same story is that he was actually referring to pornography, but it was a more polite time sixty-one years ago.)

I would draw the same parallel with workplace bullying; we may not be able to define it perfectly or even collectively, but we should all know it when we see it. My colleague Catherine Mattice is the founder and CEO of

Civility Partners, a San Diego, California–based consultancy specializing in workplace bullying prevention and conflict resolution. When I interviewed her for my "The Act of Violence" blog at Psychology Today ("Bullying in the Workplace," July 10, 2013),[2] she defined workplace bullying as creating a "psychological power imbalance, with 'horrible, willful, malicious, intentional conduct,' that fails the 'reasonable employer, supervisor, or employee test.'" This type of workplace misconduct includes yelling, threatening someone, or threatening his or her job. It could include hazing, taunting, pranks, sabotage of work or personal property. As a result, employees feel one-down, humiliated, embarrassed, driven to tears, or belittled in front of others on a regular basis. More subtle forms of bullying might be: setting employees up to fail, withholding information, negative evaluations, piling on extra work, giving the employee no work or busy work, setting impossible goals, or similar passive-aggressive behaviors.

Here's the problem with the concept of workplace bullying. Unlike sexual or racial harassment, or other forms of harassment connected to Title VII (Civil Rights Act of 1964), it is not illegal in the United States to be a bully. Individual organizations should create their own anti-bullying policies and if you need help with the language, consider adopting policies similar to what K–12 schools use and modifying that language to fit adults working in an organization. (I have sung this song for years: we need anti-bullying policies in the workplace; they should be created, released, and enforced by HR.)

SOME ADDITIONAL HELP

For your convenience, in the appendix, I have added a collection of the typical training slides I use when I teach harassment awareness, prevention, and response to general employee audiences. Customize these as you see fit.

NOTES

1. Staff written. (2023, February). Library Salaries Information. American Library Association. https://www.ala.org/educationcareers/employment/salaries.

2. Albrecht, S. (2013, July 10). Bullying in the Workplace. Psychology Today. https://www.psychologytoday.com/us/blog/the-act-of-violence/201307/bullying-in -the-workplace.

Chapter 10

Promotions, Mentoring, and Succession Planning

A soon-to-be retiring company leader said to me, with feeling, "I built this team, this department, and this organization from the ground up. I don't want someone to come in and let my baby play with razor blades."

Seems like a ringing endorsement for the value of succession planning, eh?

WHY DOESN'T EVERY EMPLOYEE WANT TO PROMOTE?

In my view, career development and career advancement are two different things, and HR plays an important role in both. The former helps employees who want to promote, at whatever level they want to achieve, by exposing them to every opportunity to grow their internal résumés, get help to move with skill through the selection and interview processes, and then launch into their new roles with the hope of both early success and the desire to stay with the organization. I see career advancement as including those elements, but being more oriented around a mentorship process—either formal or informal—that fully prepares the advancing employee into a leadership role that will satisfy their career concerns and fill pending or future gaps in the library's organizational chart. Here, the focus is on the long-term and to use the various resources to provide employees the chance to grow. One frustrating part of this version is that some managers and supervisors can't understand why some employees seem rather nonchalant about their bosses' efforts to help them advance. Why? Because some employees are perfectly happy where they are and may not welcome the move out of their comfort zone. That's fine and we need people to want to do their work where they are.

BUILDING YOUR SUCCESSION PLAN: MENTORING
AND NEW RESPONSIBILITIES

There is a view that since some public-sector organizations tend to have less of a competitive nature than for-profit, private companies, when it comes to the need to actually concentrate on succession planning as a business goal they fall short. "When the Director (#1) retires, the Assistant/Deputy/Associate Director (#2) will just step into her or his role." This thinking, while well-meaning, ignores several concerns: the first being that while the #2 might be a great person, she or he does not have the skillset for the library director's role; deep down inside, she or he doesn't really want the job, and has perhaps even hinted indirectly about it, and if nominated, won't accept it for a variety of reasons related to the stress of the job, the increased amount of community interaction and increased amount of stakeholders that demand attention, and they would prefer to stay as the #2. I have seen #2's described by themselves or by others as having great logistical skills, an operational mindset, and not-great people skills. They are great with running the library day-to-day, keeping the facility open and safe, and making sure the Internet always works. They enjoy working with the department heads and vendors, but can't stand dealing with patron complaints, community concerns, HR issues with difficult employees, and the library board.

It's easy to make the initial or ongoing assumption that the #2 is the most logical candidate to take over, since this person works closely with the #1 and as such, should know the rigors and requirements of the job. This is disproven when the #2 boldly accepts the new role and, despite a brave face, soon discovers or demonstrates that she or he is woefully unprepared for it. Just as difficult is when the #2 grudgingly steps into the new position, is instantly miserable, and leaves or demotes soon after. These both are expensive, time-consuming, and painful realizations.

There's another interesting phenomenon that often occurs during succession planning and this complaint comes from the employees. It starts usually at the entry level/staff level, but I have heard it all the way through the chain of command as well: "My boss doesn't know how to do my job! How can she or he possibly be in charge of me or others if she or he doesn't know what I do or how I do it?"

This is flawed thinking. The CEO of Boeing doesn't know every step that goes into building a commercial jet. But he or she had better know whom to hire, at every level, who does. The chief of medical staff at a hospital is certainly not an expert in every possible medical or surgery specialty, but he or she can and will rely on those individual experts and specific departments for their respective expertise. (I heard someone complain that the head of Disney only cares about boosting the stock price. I said, "Yes, you're correct, especially since that's what his Board of Directors cares about, even more than managing theme parks and making movies and TV shows.")

Good bosses at every level manage people and projects with skill, tact, and discretion. The library director may have IT, HR, Collections, Genealogy, and Facilities working for her or him. No need to be an absolute expert in each department. Just hire the right people to supervise those who do. Don't hesitate to explain this to employees and correct them, when they make their claim that just because their bosses don't known every facet of their particular jobs, somehow they are not worthy of the position.

Succession Planning should always be a mission-critical, HR-driven practice, and an important part of strategic planning and future forecasting. Library leaders must recognize the value of such planning, create a process to get it started, and ask for help from library managers and supervisors at every level to keep it going for the months and even years that it requires. And while most non-HR-oriented leaders understand the value of succession planning, they may not always participate with complete enthusiasm. It becomes one of those common "we'll cross that bridge when we come to it" time management issues, which means it's often both a rushed and an incomplete process.

Succession planning offers a process to continually assess the library's current and potential leadership talent, where HR and the leaders work to identify possible successors, and then provide those staff members with the training, mentoring, and support they need to prepare themselves for critical roles within the library organization when vacancies occur.

A library organization's succession development plan is self-investment and pre-planning for both the near-term and the future. You may need to fill a leadership role next week or in about three years. It's not uncommon for library departments to lose clusters of key personnel in short time periods, especially in today's changing work climate. Such personnel often include senior staff members and department heads. Losing them over a short period of time can create a huge hole in the library's institutional knowledge. There aren't as many skilled, steadying, and experienced leaders around to run things. As one of Ernest Hemingway's characters said in his 1926 novel, *The Sun Also Rises*, "How did you go bankrupt?" Bill asked. "Two ways," Mike said. "Gradually and then suddenly."[1]

An effective succession plan maintains an organizational state of operational readiness while it fills positions with internal candidates who are ready, willing, and able to assume the role of capable and effective leaders. Can we also go outside the library to hire for these new roles? Of course. That suggests we have neither the time nor the inclination to develop our leaders from within or if the talent pool is lacking. So the question becomes: Can we grow our new library leaders in time to meet the demand?

THE NEED FOR A SUCCESSION PLAN COORDINATOR

Guess who is the perfect person to be in charge of your library's succession plan efforts? Yes, thank you for nominating yourself. As the designated keeper of the keys for the people side of your enterprise, you are in the best position to coordinate the other leaders in the library to help you create a formal program and put it in place. You can either fine-tune an existing succession plan that exists now or start fresh. Either way, someone has to be in charge and HR is the logical place for it.

The library HR director or manager should serve as the Succession Plan Coordinator to manage and carry out the objectives of the program. (I realize this is another task on your to-do list, but it's an important one.):

- Organize and provide program oversight.
- Ensure total program top-down commitment from all library leaders at every level.
- Survey the staff to forecast potential retirement dates or personnel changes for other reasons (maternity leave, going back to school, taking a sabbatical from work, moving away, etc.).
- Serve as the primary liaison between all participants in the program.
- Facilitate coaching and mentorship training, keep meetings on the leaders' calendars, attend scheduled events as necessary, and approve the overall learning agenda for leadership development programs at all levels.
- Create and maintain program records.
- Continually update training subjects and build a collection of leadership development resources for both the mentors and the mentees.
- Provide regular updates and program status to the library director.

LIBRARY LEADERSHIP STAFF MEETINGS

A portion of the regularly scheduled staff meetings with the library leaders should dedicate some of the meeting time to discuss succession planning activities, which could include:

- Current status and updates presented by you in your HR role.
- Identification and discussion of staff members who might serve as potential leaders for future leadership positions, including which jobs and by when, if departure deadlines are looming.
- Overview of meetings, training, and mentoring completed since the last meeting.
- Prioritizing the most relevant subjects for staff development.

SUCCESSION PLAN TALENT SELECTION AND DEVELOPMENT

The selection criterion for participation in this program to select new managers might consist of:

- A minimum of three years of service as a library supervisor.
- The supervisor's last two performance evaluations must be at "Standard" and preferably "Above Standard."
- Candidates shall be identified and selected for succession development, in part, through staff's identification during leadership-level staff meetings with HR and the library director or her or his designee. Selection is based on the collective overall appraisal by the majority of the leadership team. Consideration criteria might include:
  - The supervisor's time in service.
  - The diversity of assignments by branch location, experience in supervisory tasks, and meeting the core competencies of a library supervisor.
  - Formal education, certifications, and noteworthy in-service and outside training.
  - The supervisor's expressed interest in advancing. (In other words, you can bring the horse to water, but you can't make it drink.)
- Interested supervisors should be told to submit a memo of interest to HR, detailing their interest in being considered for succession planning support and fully participating in a mentoring program.
- The library department heads or managers can notify HR to add one or more of their current supervisors to the list of possible candidates.

FOR SOON-TO-BE LIBRARY PICS: BECOME THE PIC FOR A DAY

When the work schedule is above minimum staffing levels, selected library staff employees should be given the opportunity to serve as a person in charge (PIC) for an entire shift. The acting PIC will be shadowed continually by the shift PIC, who will serve as a guide and assist the acting PIC throughout the shift.

The acting PIC will respond to employees' requests for help on the floor, handle the usual patron communications that might require a PIC, and supervise the library personnel on that shift. Qualified staff who desire the PIC role should be allowed to perform the acting PIC duties enough times to build their comfort in that new role.

Along with formal and informal coaching discussions from the current PIC or a supervisor or manager, the future PIC needs access to a collection of gradable training courses designed to develop a potential PIC's knowledge, skills, and abilities, to best assist her or him to supervise other library employees in that capacity. Training in the following areas might include:

- De-escalation skills with problematic patrons.
- Conflict resolution training between employees.
- Emergency procedures in the library (fire, evacuation, first-aid, workplace violence).
- Opening and closing time procedures.
- Dealing with vendors, board members, and elected officials as a frontline representative of the library.
- IT-related problem-solving for staff and patrons.
- Decision-making help under stress; help with problem-solving skills.
- Stress management tools and tips.

FOR SOON-TO-BE LIBRARY SUPERVISORS: BECOME THE SUPERVISOR FOR A DAY

Like becoming a PIC for several shifts, being a first-line supervisor means the current PIC now takes on the role of supervising a group of several people, beyond those who work on the library floor. This person should already have the PIC's duties under her or his belt by this career stage.

In your HR hierarchy, the supervisor's role may have the responsibilities of coaching, discipline, performance evaluations, setting work schedules, and assigning work duties and deadlines. (In some libraries, many of these performance oversight roles may only be done by a manager.)

- The full role of a library supervisor.
- Understanding risk management.
- Coaching skills for supervisors.
- Progressive discipline processes.
- How to write performance evaluations and brief their employees on them.
- Realistic time management tools and tips.

FOR SOON-TO-BE LIBRARY MANAGERS

Along with knowing how to serve the role and duties of the PICs and the supervisors, potential library managers may need these skills as well:

- The differences between "managership" (day-to-day tasks, setting and meeting deadlines, getting the best work quality out of staff, handling conflicts) and leadership (future focus, strategic planning, and broad-based thinking).
- Organizational ethics and guidelines.
- Understanding the employee workplace culture.
- Managing and/or presenting training programs that benefit employees.
- Recognizing governmental political relationships, agendas (both overt and covert), and navigating those encounters for career success.
- Risk management functions, including facilities operations.
- Understanding potential civil liabilities in publicly accessed facilities.
- Employee rights and/or union agreements during HR-related investigations.
- Budgets and fiscal operations.
- Public speaking and enhanced presentation skills; presenting to community groups, the media, and electeds.

FOR SOON-TO-BE LIBRARY DEPARTMENT HEADS, LIBRARY ASSISTANT DIRECTORS, DEPUTY DIRECTORS, OR ASSOCIATE DIRECTORS

- The role of the library department head (including serving as the acting or interim library director, if necessary).
- Knowing all facets of tangible library day-to-day operations (which should be outlined in an operations manual that gets updated).
- Administrative and executive expectations of the library department head, by the library director, library boards, and elected officials.
- Scanning and forecasting: developing the library's strategic plan.
- Budget responsibilities.
- Grant writing and capital improvement bonds for facility growth, additional branches, and building enhancements.
- Mentoring and coaching current and future managers and supervisors.
- Running department head meetings.
- Regular meetings with HR, Facilities, IT, and the library's legal advisor.

FOR SOON-TO-BE LIBRARY DIRECTORS

Once it's clear the current library director has an end date, potential replacement candidates should meet these criteria (and other skills, as determined by HR, the library board, and other stakeholders):

- A pattern of executive development, leadership skills, and continuing education.
- Knowing and implementing the role of the library director in a community.
- Fiscal management.
- Organizational team-building at all levels.
- Media management and relations.
- Knowing and implementing the role of the library director in city/county government operations.
- Awareness of the current and future political environments (existing and new city council or county supervisor members, library board members).
- Developing and achieving the library's strategic plan.

As the selection process for the next potential library director narrows, that candidate should get further insight into the current director's routine, network, contacts, information sources, media sources, budget discretion, operational protocols, and benefit from the outgoing library director's shared experience.

(My thanks to my Southern California leadership colleague, Andrew Borrello, for his contribution to my knowledge on succession planning for this chapter.)

HR HELP: CHALLENGES FOR NEW BOSSES

Being a new supervisor can get overwhelming. So much to do, so little time (at least that's a common perception), and so many small fires and occasional big blazes to put out. It can help to see challenges as more like opportunities, instead of always as obstacles.

My coaching conversations with new bosses often come after they have been doing their new work for six months to one year. We discuss the issues and events they have experienced that make their job both difficult and rewarding. It can be frustrating to have certain expectations and either not meet them or feel let down by people above or below you, who don't share your same energy or enthusiasm. It's often tough to navigate office politics, flawed policies, outdated systems, embedded bureaucracies, and decision chokepoints.

This collection of six challenges seems to be the ones most often voiced by new supervisors. They can and need to be turned into opportunities to do better, smarter work, on behalf of the organization, their bosses, other bosses, other departments, their staff (whether they supervise one person or thirty), and the patrons they all serve. Your role in HR is to help them address these.

Quote these sections to them as you need to (this is you talking to them):

Addressing Repeated Attendance Problems

"Perhaps somewhat surprisingly, this is a consistent complaint from new supervisors: 'Why can't my employees get to work on time, start on time, manage their breaks and lunches correctly, and leave on time? I don't want to have to adjust work schedules because people come in late and try to make up the time.' Instead of allowing employees to come and go as they want, we need every member of the boss's team to follow the same rules as every other department in the organization. The library HR department will not want to have to defend against a wage and hour civil suit that arises because a group of employees claims they weren't paid fairly and accurately. It can help to print out the library policy on attendance—for both hourly and salaried employees—and talk about it in detail at an all-hands staff meeting. The time to start enforcing this is now."

Managing Your New Boss

"It may sound selfish, but in terms of career success and survival, you must put the needs of your boss first, balance the needs of your team second, and then focus on the needs of each employee third. Your boss should get the most attention because he or she has a different set of priorities, which will need to be met, for the overall success of the department. He or she will have high expectations for the delegated projects you have been given. Your boss's success starts with your ability to understand what needs to be done, even when it's not always completely clear. You'll have to set a balance between too many clarification meetings and not enough, to get the directions you need. It's not that you ignore the requests and concerns of your staff, but you need to keep your eye on your larger responsibilities."

Supervising Former Colleagues

"This challenge often takes two forms: your pal now works for you and expects an easier path since you're friends, or one of your colleagues, who is not a fan of yours, didn't get the promotion you got and may decide not to work very hard on your behalf. Either situation can harm the pace and quality of work and must be addressed using one or more coaching meetings before things get out of hand. To your friend, you need to say, 'I know we go back a bit and have a good relationship at work and outside of work. I want to be able to count on you to do your work and the things I ask you to do. We can still be friends even though I'm your boss, but I have to know I can depend on you.'

"To the former colleague who harbors a grudge, you can say, 'I know you put in for this job and you may have some strong feelings that I got it. I've always respected your work ability and job knowledge. I want to be able to count on you to do your work and the things I ask you to do. I hope we can improve our relationship going forward.' Different versions of the same speech, with the same goal. Use a firm, fair, and consistent supervisory style with both. Be sure to write accurate performance evaluations and coach each equally; you don't want to be accused of favoritism or punishment.

"The other three here are more complex, time-intensive, and mission-critical. They will require some study, a focus on both short-term tasks and longer-term goals, and a willingness to pay attention to what makes a successful work culture."

Staying Compliant with HR Policies and Legal Requirements

"Keeping current on ever-changing personnel and related legal issues can no longer be seen as the job of just your HR colleagues. The courthouses are filled with civil employment claims, ranging from harassment, disparate treatment, and Americans with Disabilities Act (ADA) accommodations, to employee safety hazards, retaliation for whistleblowing, and employee leave/benefit claims related to the Family Medical Leave Act (FMLA). It's a lot to know.

"Have the courage and good sense to know what you know about labor law policies and personnel issues. Introduce yourself to your HR department representatives. Develop an information-gathering and problem-solving relationship with one of your HR specialists, who can keep you apprised of emerging trends, new case laws, and supervisory best practices. Sign up for HR-related websites, like the Society for Human Resource Management (SHRM.org), the largest HR association in the world. Set up Google notices in your email to get stories and examples of new HR case law, especially involving your type of company and employees (union or non-union; blue-collar or white-collar). There are many national and local law firms that practice HR-related law and who will provide your managers and supervisors with monthly newsletters that discuss legislation in your state and examples from recent court cases, most often of what not to do. If you are in a union shop, they must read and at least be familiar with all employee association and union Memos of Understanding (MOUs). One of your roles in HR is to know how and when to get them legal advice. And they must have the courage to bring potential employee problems to your attention early rather than late.

"Two of the most common legal questions related to employer liability are these: 'When did you become aware of this issue? What was your response?'

Employee legal problems rarely solve themselves or go away without senior management intervention. Use your HR team as an educational component and as leverage to stay effective and legal."

Managing New and Existing Projects to Meet Quality Needs and Deadlines

"Realize how critically important it is to manage people, projects, and outcomes, in the proper order of priority that matches the need premise and the situation. Encourage your managers and supervisors to install and use a physical, centrally located big project board. Their employees should know what is ongoing, pending, due, overdue, and what they can help others do. They should not hesitate to assign people by name to specific delegated tasks; visibility helps with accountability. They need to be ready to coach their employees in private for issues related to missing deadlines, poor quality work, and not keeping work output promises made to them and the team. They need to post the long-term project list and a short-term project list on the Big Board. There should be no moments where their employees wander around with a cup of coffee, not sure as to what they need to do next. They need to reward their successes but not allow critical work not to get done. The all-purpose employee excuse—'Sorry, I ran out of time and didn't do it,' is not acceptable. If they are struggling, encourage your managers and supervisors to come to you before important project deadlines loom. You may be able to help them split up the tasks, get them more help, provide guidance or training, and still meet the deadline."

Supporting a Positive Employee Work Culture

"Employees stay in jobs where they feel supported, valued, heard, and praised. In these current times of unfilled jobs, labor shortages, and underemployment, how we treat people matters. The supervisory style in your library plays a big part in the health of your organization's work culture, which can be perceived by employees as either toxic or nourishing, both overall and in their department. Seek to understand by listening more and talking less. Your employees already know you are in charge; you don't have to lecture them or demonstrate the micromanaging Knowledge Curse (telling them how to do things, in detail, that they already know how to do). Test employee complaints for truth: observe, verify, and ask. Don't be afraid to fix what's always been broken by eliminating processes or revamping inefficient organizational policies that are not value-added and waste your employees' time and efforts. Make small, useful changes fast; make big sweeping changes over time. Use more praise."

Time to Get Back to Recognizing and Rewarding Your Employees

One value of specialization is that when you become really good at what you do, people seek you out. Doctors, lawyers, and your plumber prove this all the time. Bob Nelson is the internationally recognized guru on employee recognition and rewards. For decades, he has been developing ways for business owners, leaders, managers, and supervisors to catch their people doing the right things since the publication of his book, *1001 Ways to Reward Employees.*[2]

That book, which sold over 1.4 million copies and spawned several sequels, was one of the first business books to recognize that rewarding employees was not only worthwhile, but even kinda fun. Nelson studied employee motivation for his PhD and began to tell business leaders what we all know today: workers come to work for more than just the paycheck. It's how they are *treated* that matters most.

Every study and survey on employee motivation always comes to the same conclusion: pay is *an* important factor in why an employee chooses to join an organization, but not *the* primary motivator. And how new employees are treated from Day One, as part of a skilled, organized (not haphazard), and thorough onboarding and orientation process, goes a long way to helping them stay and work hard while they are there.

Consider your own career. You have certainly worked at jobs where you weren't paid much but still enjoyed the work, the culture, and your co-workers. Some of us have worked in jobs where the pay was good but the culture, the working conditions, and how we were treated drove us to quit. Many of us have worked hard at volunteer jobs where we didn't get a dime and we did it because we loved it, wanted to give back to our community, or cherished the ability to support and be with our kids. Getting involved in grassroots community projects, helping out at your church, or coaching your children's sports teams are all examples where what we do is not driven by an economic reward.

There are still certain business owners or leaders who believe that employees only work, or, at least, only work hard for a paycheck. This ongoing belief may be connected to the reality that in the current economy, with WFH now the norm, some workers are in no rush to return to work.

Reviewing Bob Nelson's books on employee motivation and rewards, several themes emerge. Like an army, the workforce is contented by a full stomach. Food is a powerful motivator. Prisons rioted and old navies mutinied when the chow was terrible. The popularity of gift baskets, restaurant gift cards, bagels and coffee for everyone, pizza every other Friday, or an occasional full-catered buffet lunch, suggests that employees like free food—healthy some days, sweet, fried, and salty on others.

Random monies are a nice reward too, beyond just a year-end bonus. Amazon gift cards, Apple music cards, gas cards, operational performance bonuses, and even actual American greenbacks, are all welcome additions to employees' wish lists of rewards.

The key to any reward is to make it random, episodic, and performance-based. Donuts every Monday is boring after the third week. The same reward every quarter is predictable and shows no imagination. Plan your employee rewards program like it was a Las Vegas slot machine; it pays off when the person least expects it. Be fair—don't always recognize the same rising stars. Be objective—one or more employees should not be rewarded for something others do every day.

Employee rewards and recognition efforts need a public element too. One of Bob Nelson's surveys about what works suggested that public praise of an employee, led by a senior company leader, and done in front of the whole firm, had a lasting and positive impact. When an employee says, "Don't make a big deal, I was just doing my job," that's your signal to put together a ceremony and provide that person with a symbol that shows your gratitude for doing that job with skill.

Your formalized employee recognition should reflect what your supervisors and staff have done for each other and your patrons over the year. Sit down with your leadership team and brainstorm the world of recognition and reward possibilities you can create, that are feasible, budget-friendly, and most of all, creative. Let's get back to celebrating our workplace accomplishments, in small and big ways. Let's realize the value of the R's and the C's.

Rituals.
Rewards.
Recognition.

Celebrations.
Ceremonies.
Commitment to Excellence.

Good luck!

NOTES

1. Hemingway, Ernest. (1926). *The Sun Also Rises*. Scribner's.
2. Nelson, Bob. (1994). *1,001 Ways to Reward Your Employees* (1st ed.). Workman Publishing.

Appendix

A FEW WORDS ABOUT HR INFORMATION SYSTEMS (HRIS) SOFTWARE

If I have a knowledge gap in HR (besides not having memorized every legal decision), it would be what I know and don't know about HRIS—Human Resources Information Systems software program. On its face, these programs offer a one-stop shop for all your HR needs, helping you track, organize, and activate the entire employment cycle for screening, assessing résumés, developing interviewing strategies, and managing each employees' e-file through probation, discipline, PIPs and BIPs, any workers' compensation or medical injuries, FMLA or ADA accommodations, copies of their performance evaluations, benefits packages, terminations, and even retirements.

These programs are modularized, based on your employee size and record-keeping needs. You can scale them up as you grow (with the accompanying price increase for the yearly site license, to be sure).

The primary value for me—besides the obvious convenience in the HR record keeping and activation of the various modules through the employment lifespan—is the security of the data. No other entity in an organization keeps as much personal, proprietary data as HR. We are the custodians of an employee's medical benefits information, date of birth, Social Security number, children's names, home address, emergency contact, insurance beneficiaries, and salary information.

What used to be kept in file cabinets (sometimes half-rusted, sometimes only occasionally locked) is now in the cloud. This is significant, today and back then, to not only guarantee a sense of peace of mind to the employee but also to be able to say to an attorney—ours or theirs, in a wage and hour dispute, unlawful termination, harassment, discrimination, or retaliation lawsuit—that we protected the information from its first arrival into our office.

Electronic discovery of HR records is serious business. I once sat through a ninety-minute conference workshop presented by two labor law attorneys and what I heard is that every document that is date-stamped and time-stamped is evaluated by both sides as to who accessed it, when, where, why, and how. (I'll admit the only reason I watched their session was because I had to. I was the previous presenter and had left my cell phone on the podium where they were speaking. I couldn't have just strolled up to the dais and picked it up, in front of the whole room, and interrupted their session, now could I?)

The point is e-discovery is a real thing, and you protect your library and your reputation as an HR professional by having a pristine and bulletproof HR documents management. Your HRIS software needs to use state-of-the-art login procedures. We never want to explain to our employees how their personal information was exposed due to internal or external hacking.

A word about WFH when it comes to HR activities. First, perhaps you're fully familiar with attorneys and document discovery. As a precursor to the litigation process, your library in general and you in particular could be served with a civil order (called in some states a "subpoena duces tecum") demanding all records for a particular employee during a certain period. This is a court order for "the production of evidence, ordering the recipient to appear before the court and produce documents or other tangible evidence for use at a hearing or trial." This means in a labor law civil suit, they will ask for everything involving the employee(s) suing (the plaintiff[s]) or the employer being sued (the defendant library, the city or county that operates the library, the library board, variously named managers, supervisors, or employees, the library director, the HR director, etc.).

Be careful how you "co-mingle" your at-work work activities with your at-home work activities. An example: You are working from your library office on an employee discipline package or a performance evaluation. You quit for the day and before you leave, you email yourself the documents so you can work on them at home. If you download those documents to your at-work assigned laptop, which you bring back and forth from your home office to your work office, you're fine. If you download those documents to a desktop at home—either given to you by your employer for that sole purpose or you bought your own at-home desktop, solely for work tasks—you're fine.

If you use your home laptop, desktop, or tablet (and maybe even your personal, non-work-provided smartphone) for both your personal life and your professional life, you could get some unwanted scrutiny on those devices. Although it's rare, the other side's attorney can be a stickler about your mixing work and personal materials, because when they ask for "all HR documents related to the employee in question from the date of hire until date of termination," and you don't provide enough and they believe you are hiding something, they could, in theory, get a court order to have a forensic computer examiner do a full audit of your home and work devices.

While this may seem to you and me to be highly intrusive and an invasion of your privacy, I have seen this happen to HR directors and managers. If all you have on your at-home computer is some of your grandma's candy recipes, you might not mind if some technician creates a written report of everything that's on your hard drive for the other side's review. If you're like the rest of us, with our whole lives on those boxes, you certainly have the right to feel put upon.

The solution to preventing this forensic intrusion is simple: leave your work at work or only open work-related files on home devices that are solely for that purpose.

THE HR POLICY POSTER ALPHABET

Ah, the collection of posters our federal and state governments require us to hang in a visible location at the work site. Ranging from EEOC guidelines; to the Polygraph Protection Act (that one doesn't seem to come up all that often); the Family Medical Leave Act (FMLA); the Americans with Disabilities (ADA) Act; the Age Discrimination Employment Act (ADEA); union Memos of Understanding (MOUs); sick leave policies; workers' compensation rights; and the historical but still necessary sexual harassment reporting guidelines, these big paper sheets tell our employees a lot.

If you haven't updated your posters in a few years, you can and should go to the Internet and order a fresh set from the various HR suppliers that address both the specific standards from the feds and your state as well. (Some companies that provide these printed resources will put you on a subscription plan, meaning they will automatically send you updated posters as federal and your state laws change.)

And while I get the need for the plethora of posters in the employee break room, it is our function in HR to be able to accurately interpret those requirements and more importantly, be able to explain what is what and why is why to our employees. As you stand with a cup of coffee in hand, staring at the wall display, could you summarize the contents of each to a group of new employees, in a way that helps them know their rights and responsibilities?

By rights, I mean what they should be expected to know about a specific HR area, as to how and why they are protected. And by responsibilities, they should know from you—and your written policies and the work culture you are trying to create and nurture—that they have to tell you when those rights are in jeopardy. Your message to every employee should be: "We can't fix what we don't know about. You must have the assertiveness and even the courage to tell your department heads, managers, supervisors, and PICs, or any of us in Human Resources, when there are issues, conflicts, problems, or personal boundary violations we need to address on your behalf. Don't wait until the problem grows to double in size. Most things with bosses, co-workers, or patrons can be addressed, explained, or corrected, if we know about them soonest."

SAMPLE TRAINING SLIDES FOR A HARASSMENT AWARENESS, PREVENTION, AND RESPONSE PROGRAM

Perhaps you already have a recorded in-service training program on hand, or you use one of your library trainers, or you bring in an outside HR consultant to do these sessions. You might even be the one who teaches this subject for your library, both as a new hire, onboarding, new employee orientation process, and as a regular reminder to all staff, managers, and supervisors (a reasonable thing to do annually). If you need to turn what I have provided here into a full slide set or you just want to pick and choose some key concepts to add to your existing material, please do.

I have taught this type of program, most often for California cities, counties, and libraries, for several decades. I mention California because the legislators started to specifically address sexual and racial harassment in 2004, when Governor Arnold Schwarzenegger signed Assembly Bill 1825 mandating sexual harassment training for nearly every public sector and private sector employer in the state. (I'm aware of the irony of Arnold signing such a bill, based on his highly public marital issues.)

At first, AB 1825 required the training for agency leaders, managers, and supervisors only, then it added all employees, and then it added all elected/appointed officials (who also have to take a mandated ethics training class too). The State of California then added a concept the lawmakers (poorly) defined as "abusive conduct," which is (kinda, sorta) about workplace bullying. My point here is that your state may have some specific laws or suggested guidelines about sexual and racial harassment as a required training subject. Make certain you are up to date on their training standards for your library.

You'll note this section's title: "Harassment Awareness, Prevention, and Response" is to tell all employees the importance of these three elements: we want you to be aware of this subject, including your rights as an employee and your responsibilities as a manager or supervisor; we will do all we can, collectively, to prevent these types of behaviors from happening to any employee, full-time, part-time, or volunteer; and we want all employees to know, at every level, that we have a response protocol in place that includes an initial assessment of the complaint and an investigation that includes conversations with the targeted employee, the perpetrator (if it is an employee or even a patron), and any bystander witnesses, who can corroborate what they saw or heard.

The final part of our investigative response will be a report, as detailed as necessary, to include consequences for perpetrators (employees, vendors, contractors, patrons) and support for targeted employees (time off, access to EAP counseling, requesting a transfer to another branch, or into a different no-patron-contact role, etc.).

Use these slides for your library and state-specific harassment training program. Add or subtract from them or delete those that don't apply to your library or your state.

Slide 1: EXPECTATIONS FROM THE EQUAL EMPLOYMENT OPPORTUNITY COMMISSION (EEOC)

Leadership and accountability.

Anti-harassment policies.

Harassment reporting systems and investigations.

Compliance training

Retaliation is the number one issue addressed by the EEOC—54 percent of their cases.

Slide 2: WHY ARE WE HERE?

This is an important part of your employment here. We have policies and expectations about fair treatment of all employees: you have the right to work in a harassment-free environment. We will address this issue as soon as you bring it to our attention, offering support for targeted employees and consequences for perpetrators.

Besides sexual harassment, the training should cover preventing discrimination or harassment based on race, color, national origin, ancestry, religion, disabilities, medical condition, family or pregnancy leave, gender, gender expression, marital status, sexual orientation, age, or any other legally protected classes in our state.

Slide 3: TRAINING REQUIREMENTS

This training will provide "effective, interactive, informative, practical guidance, covering relevant federal and state laws."

We will fully explain our library's prohibitions against sexual and racial harassment, and the prevention and correction methods.

We will provide definitions and practical examples to teach leaders, managers, and supervisors to recognize harassment, discrimination, and retaliation.

We will describe the remedies available to targeted employees.

We will provide a copy of the library's harassment policy to all training participants.

Slide 4: HERE'S THE GOOD NEWS . . .

No role plays or embarrassing skits.

No boring, controversial, or outdated videos.

No rehashing of past situations here.

No hitting you over the head with "The Law Book."

Just the right information to keep our library organization in compliance and to provide you with the tools to be an ethical, smart, and productive leader, manager, supervisor, or an informed employee.

Slide 5: THE NEW WORKPLACE

An ever-growing diversity of people, cultures, religions, sexual orientations, opinions, beliefs, tolerances, and generations.

Slide 6: DEFINING THE "HOSTILE WORK ENVIRONMENT"

Treatment based on being in a protected class.

Treatment that interferes with an employee's ability to do his or her job successfully.

Could be created by bosses or co-workers.

Must be discriminatory in nature. Severe, pervasive, retaliatory, not stopped by management.

Context is critical; hurt feelings, rude people, and overly assertive bosses do not meet the legal definition.

Slide 7: TYPICAL PROTECTED CLASSES

race

color

national origin / ancestry

religion

physical or mental disability
medical condition
accommodation requests
pregnancy, breastfeeding, family care
veteran status
gender or gender identity
political affiliations
domestic violence victims
genetic information
marital status
sexual orientation
age

Slide 8: "AGE DIVERSITY"

Some workplace conflicts between employees have nothing to do with sexual or racial harassment or any lighter protected class issue. Sometimes people just don't get along because of differences in their ages, where they just see their world differently. If you disagree with a colleague, might it be because of an age gap, where your perceptions are completely different than theirs?

Baby Boomers (1946 to 1964)
Generation X (1965 to 1980)
Generation Y (1981 to 1999)
Generation Z (2000 to now)

Slide 9: SEXUAL OR RACIAL HARASSMENT 101

"Unwelcome, hostile, offensive, severe, intimidating, interfering, pervasive, repetitive"

Any visual, verbal, or physical conduct based on sex or of a sexual nature, race, or other protected classes that unreasonably interferes with a person's job performance; submission is used as a condition of employment; or creates a hostile, offensive, or abusive workplace atmosphere.

One incident may or may not qualify as a violation, depending on the severity.

Slide 10: SEXUALLY HOSTILE WORK ENVIRONMENTS

Sexually oriented or gender-based jokes, comments, photos, cartoons, electronic images, public remarks.

Intentional rubbing, touching, or blocking the path of a person. Leering, ogling, sexually oriented looks and gestures. No sexual gratification is necessary (which was a former "defense" by some perpetrators).

Comments or gossip about sexual activities, or negative comments about sexual orientation.

Showing favoritism to those who allow or engage in harassing behaviors, or allowing retaliation.

No boss–employee relationship is necessary.

Slide 11: SEXUALLY HARASSING RELATIONSHIPS
male to female
female to male
same gender harassment
harassment based on sexual orientation
third-parties (patrons, vendors, contractors, visitors)
Remember, a boss–employee relationship does not always have to exist.

Slide 12: RACIALLY HOSTILE WORK ENVIRONMENTS
Racially oriented or religious-based jokes, comments, photos, cartoons, public remarks.

Discrimination based on religious beliefs, ethnicity, national origin.

May include "nicknames," teasing about accents, and similar derogatory comments.

Showing favoritism to those who allow or engage in these harassing behaviors, or allowing retaliation.

No boss–employee relationship is necessary.

Slide 13: DEFINING TWO TYPES OF SEXUAL HARASSMENT
"Quid Pro Quo"—Latin for "This for that." A library leader, manager, or supervisor asks a job applicant or an employee for sexual favors as a condition of employment. (Liability to the organization is automatic and non-defensible, even if the applicant or employee consents to the sexual relationship initially.)

"Sexually Hostile Environment"—Most common and most recognizable.

Slide 14: QUID PRO QUO HARASSMENT
Job benefits connected to receiving sexual favors, typically from a supervisor or manager, who holds the power of hiring, promotion, transfer, work duties, or work schedule over the applicant or employee.

Least common form of sexual harassment—about 5 percent of reported cases in the United States.

Can also involve female bosses and male employees, same-sex, senior executives through first-line supervisors.

Slide 15: DEFINING A "SUPERVISOR"

Per the US Supreme Court decision *Vance v. Ball State University*: "Someone who the employer vests with authority to direct and oversee an employee's daily work. He or she has the power to hire, fire, demote, promote, evaluate, transfer, or discipline the employee."

Slide 16: OUR THEMES

Sexual and racial harassment prevention is everyone's responsibility. We respect each other's boundaries here.

Our organization will not tolerate any form of harassment.

All leaders, managers, and supervisors must work to create and model a harassment-free workplace. We provide multiple channels of reporting through many leadership stakeholders: HR, library director, library board, library attorney, and/or the state EEOC or Fair Employment agency.

There are consequences for any employees (or others) who violate this policy (or who make false accusations).

There is support, advice, and assistance for employees who report harassing behavior (even if they want nothing done), including protection from retaliation.

Remedies: coaching, training, requested transfer, discipline, termination.

Slide 17: THE BIG PICTURE

Since the passage of Title VII of the Civil Rights Act in 1964, federal and state employment laws entitle everyone to a workplace that is free from sexual or racial harassment.

Sexual or racial harassment is against our policy and outside the course and scope of your employment.

It will not be tolerated, and ignorance of the law or our policies, or "I was just joking" are not acceptable defenses.

Besides the potential for losing your job, you could be personally sued for sexual or racial harassment.

This is an important subject and a critical part of your employment here.

It's about respect and dignity, personal responsibility, support for targeted employees, and consequences for perpetrators.

Slide 18: OUR SEXUAL HARASSMENT POLICY

Purpose—To provide a work environment free from sexual or racial harassment.

Eligibility—All employees, patrons, vendors, contractors.

Definition—No visual, verbal, or physical harassment or offensive conduct that creates a hostile work environment and no sexually oriented harassment in any form.

Administration—Report complaints to the senior library leadership, HR, or any manager or supervisor, who will respond to every complaint, policy violation, retaliation claim, or false accusation. We will assess each situation, investigate it fully, make decisions, and enforce our policy.

Discipline—Up to and including termination.

Slide 19: RETALIATION

No adverse actions may be taken against the reporting party, perpetrators, witnesses, bystanders, or employees who participate in the investigation.

Examples: silent treatment, harsh treatment, transfers, demotions, hours change, skipping promotions, job duties change, not providing information, denial of overtime, negative performance evaluations, bad references.

Slide 20: OUR PERSONAL MOTTO . . .

"Is what I am about to do or say going to be okay with the other person?" (Using good social intelligence, read the room and then don't do it or say it.)

THE FIRST BITE OF THE APPLE *

We can all teach this to each other:

End the problem when it is small, by giving the person the chance to stop or correct his or her behavior.

If that doesn't stop the problem, go to your supervisor, the next supervisor in or out of your chain, and / or HR for more help.

* Direct confrontation is not a requirement, but it's one way to help us all self-manage this issue.

Slide 21: CAN WE DEFINE WORKPLACE BULLYING?

Yelling, threatening someone, or threatening his or her job.

"Horrible, willful, malicious, intentional conduct," that fails the "reasonable employer, supervisor, or employee test."

Creating a "psychological power imbalance," so that employees feel one-down: humiliated, embarrassed, driven to tears, or belittled in front of others, on a regular basis.

Hazing, taunting, pranks, sabotage of work or personal property.

More subtle forms: setting employees up to fail, withholding information, negative evaluations, piling on work, setting impossible goals, passive-aggressive behaviors.

Slide 22: COSTS OF BULLYING

Low morale, poor performance, distracted, fearful, emotional, anxious employees.

Creates retention problems, high turnover, and a bad reputation in the work community.

Legal costs, liability issues, higher insurance or litigation costs.

"The bullies run the workplaces and even the bosses are afraid."

A lack of management vigilance, courage, immediate and effective responses, no consequences, no support.

Not defining a tough boss versus a bullying boss, to both sides.

Slide 23: GETTING ALONG IN THE OFFICE

What is "cubicle or work station etiquette"? Always ask; never assume.

Agree on mutual privacy.

Give each other *direct* (to the person), *non-personal* (stick to the business issues), *immediate* (right now) *feedback* (ask them to stop the behavior).

Slide 24: ORGANIZATIONAL RED FLAGS

Allowing a sexually or racially harassing work culture to exist without intervention, any progressive discipline, or significant consequences for perpetrators.

Targeted employees who fear the consequences of reporting.

Covert or overt tolerance by leaders, managers, or supervisors, even after repeated events, complaints, or reports.

Failing to respond quickly, investigate, and stop the behavior.

Slide 25: THE MANAGER OR SUPERVISOR'S PROCESS

Respond immediately; listen to the complaint. Is there a history between one or more of the parties?

Contact your supervisor and/or HR immediately; support their efforts.

Did the employee stop the chain of command? If so, why?

Help identify all participants, witnesses, or evidence.

Follow "need to know" confidentiality.

Don't make false promises or ignore the issue.

Document your discussions and response steps.

Continue to monitor for retaliation.

Slide 26: TEACHING OUR EMPLOYEES TO KNOW THEIR RIGHTS

If you feel you have been sexually or racially harassed, tell the person to stop the comments or behavior.

If the person does not stop, report it immediately to your supervisor, another supervisor, and/or HR.

Don't wait until the situation escalates. Don't give the power back to the harasser by not reporting it.

Tell the truth. Provide documentation or witnesses if possible. Have patience through the investigation process. Recognize the limits of confidentiality.

Slide 27: EMAIL AND SOCIAL MEDIA USAGE ISSUES

There is no expectation of privacy on any email or Internet / Intranet correspondence. These systems are subject to management audit.

Do not show, create, or forward inappropriate emails or cell phone–based videos, photos, jokes, cartoons, memes, and so on.

Be mindful of your work-related postings on all social media sites. The Internet never forgets.

Slide 28: OUR STATE

Our State's Department of Fair Employment and Housing (DFEH) website.
The Fair Employment and Housing Act (FEHA)
Facts about sexual harassment
Employers' obligations
Employer liability
Filing a complaint
Contact information

Slide 29: DO YOUR PART TO MAKE US THE BEST WORKPLACE

Treat each other like professional co-workers and colleagues.

Respect the personal and professional boundaries of your co-workers.

Use the "first bite of the apple" concept.

Get help from your boss, HR, or another leader who can help you address the problem.

Understand, follow, model, and respect our policy.

Index

About the Author

Dr. **Steve Albrecht** is well-known to library training audiences around the country. Since 2000, he has trained thousands of library employees, live and online, in service, safety, and security. He has worked with city and county libraries, K–12 libraries, college and university libraries, special libraries, and law libraries, in over thirty states.

In 2015, the ALA published his book *Library Security: Better Communication, Safer Facilities* and in 2023, Rowman & Littlefield published his book *The Safe Library: Keeping Users, Staff, and Collections Secure.*

Steve is represented by Library 2.0 (www.Library20.com), a free library membership organization founded by Steve Hargadon, with over 60,000 members. Albrecht provides the members with free monthly podcasts, articles, paid webinars, and all-access content passes.

Steve holds a doctoral degree in business administration (DBA), an MA in security management, a BS in psychology, and a BA in English. He is board-certified in human resources, security management, employee coaching, and threat assessment.

He has written twenty-six other books on business, security, criminal justice, and leadership topics. He lives with seven dogs and two cats in Springfield, Missouri.

His website, www.TheSafeLibrary.com (co-curated with Steve Hargadon), offers free resources for library leaders and staff, including articles, recorded webinars, and examples of his training and consulting work for improved library service, safety, and security.

He can also be reached at www.DrSteveAlbrecht.com.